LIFE SKILLS FOR TWEENS:

How to Cook, Make Friends, Be Self Confident and Healthy

Everything a Pre Teen Should Know to Be a Brilliant Teenager

FERNE BOWE

SOMETHING FOR YOU!

Get your **<u>FREE</u>** Tweenage Cookbook + Bonus Worksheets

SCAN QR CODE TO GET YOUR COPY

TABLE OF CONTENTS

INTRODUCTION

Congratulations! You're about to become a teenager!

It's an exciting time, but it can also be scary. As you get older, there are many new things you have to learn and deal with. But don't worry, it's perfectly normal to feel anxious about what lies ahead.

As you move through life, you will encounter challenges and obstacles. You can overcome some of these easily, but others may seem impossible. This is where having strong life skills comes in handy. If you can problem-solve and communicate effectively, you will be better equipped to handle whatever life throws your way.

But first up, what are life skills?

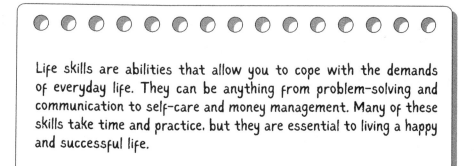

Life skills are abilities that allow you to cope with the demands of everyday life. They can be anything from problem-solving and communication to self-care and money management. Many of these skills take time and practice. but they are essential to living a happy and successful life.

Learning life skills is essential. Many of the jobs you will apply for in the future will require you to have specific life skills. For example, to be a teacher, you must communicate effectively and manage a classroom. If you're going to be an accountant, you will need to be able to manage money and keep track of financial records. So, whether you realize it or not, life skills are essential for almost everything you do.

There are many benefits to having strong life skills. Some of the most important ones are:

- You will be able to handle difficult situations with ease.
- You will be able to achieve your goals and dreams.
- You will be more confident in yourself.
- You will have better relationships with others.
- You will be able to live a happy and fulfilling life.

So, as you can see, having strong life skills is essential for a happy and successful life. To achieve your goals and dreams, you need to start working on your life skills today!

That's where this book comes in. This book is designed to help you develop the life skills you need to make the jump to a teenager. We will cover topics to help you:

- Make friends and build relationships
- Make responsible decisions
- Stay fit and live healthily
- Communicate effectively
- Set goals and achieve them
- Live a life of an adventurer

And so much more.

Each chapter will include tips, illustrations, and real-life examples to help you understand and apply the life skills we are discussing. So, let's get started!

CHAPTER 1

PERSONAL DEVELOPMENT

As you approach becoming a teenager, you will face new challenges and opportunities. These are exciting times! Even though you don't know it yet, everything you do is helping you shape who you will become. Your decisions and actions will have a massive impact on your future.

The world is your oyster, anything is possible, and you have the power to create your destiny.

But before you can conquer the world, there are some essential life skills you need to learn first. These will help you navigate through your teenage years and beyond.

Some of the things you'll need to know include:

- How to manage your time effectively
- How to set goals
- How to stay on track
- How to be confident
- How to motivate yourself

Each of these topics is important in its own right. Still, together, they will form the foundation for a happy, successful teenage experience.

So let's take a closer look at each one.

· ·
HOW TO BE A TIME MANAGEMENT SUPERSTAR

Time management is one of the most essential life skills you can learn.

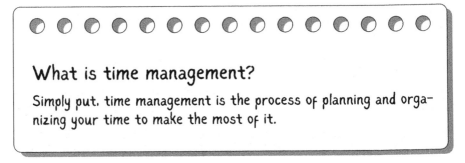

What is time management?

Simply put, time management is the process of planning and organizing your time to make the most of it.

It sounds easy enough, but it's pretty tricky to do.

There are only 24 hours in a day, and there's only so much you can fit into that time. Effective time management is all about prioritizing your time and using it wisely.

As a teenager, you'll be juggling schoolwork, extracurricular activities, socializing, and perhaps even a part-time job. You must learn to manage your time effectively, or you'll quickly become overwhelmed.

Here are some tips to help you get started:

① **Make a list of everything you need to do.** The best way to do this is to get a piece of paper and write down everything on your mind. Once it's all down on paper, you'll feel much better and see everything more clearly.

2 **Prioritize your tasks.** Once you've got everything down on paper, it's time to start working out which tasks are the most important and must be done first. This is called prioritizing.

Ask yourself the most critical task that needs to be completed first. This is usually the task with the most significant consequences if it's not done or the most urgent one. For example, from the list above, doing your homework, or walking the dog, would be more important than playing football with your friends.

Put a number 1 next to the most important task. Then ask yourself, what is the second most important task? Put a number 2 next to that one. Continue doing this until you've numbered all of your tasks.

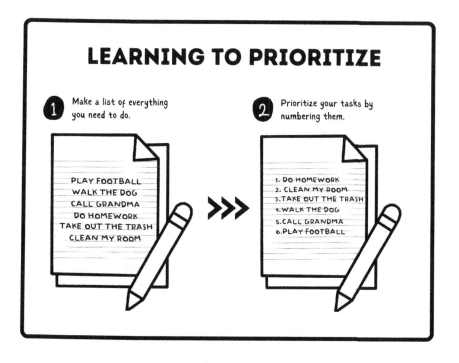

LEARNING TO PRIORITIZE

1 Make a list of everything you need to do.

PLAY FOOTBALL
WALK THE DOG
CALL GRANDMA
DO HOMEWORK
TAKE OUT THE TRASH
CLEAN MY ROOM

2 Prioritize your tasks by numbering them.

1. DO HOMEWORK
2. CLEAN MY ROOM
3. TAKE OUT THE TRASH
4. WALK THE DOG
5. CALL GRANDMA
6. PLAY FOOTBALL

3 **Create a plan.** Once you know what needs to be done and in what order, you can start creating a plan. This can be as simple as writing down what you need to do and when you need to do it.

4 **Get to work.** Now that you've planned everything out, it's time to start working on your tasks. The best way to do this is to start with the most important task and work your way down the list. This will help you ensure that the most important things get done first.

5 **Take breaks.** It's essential to take breaks while you're working on tasks. This will help you to avoid burnout and will keep your mind fresh.

6 **Stick to your plan.** Once you've created your program, do your best to stick to it. This means setting aside specific times for specific tasks and then making sure you actually do those tasks during that time.

. . . .

HOW TO SET GOALS

Setting goals is another skill you'll need to learn as a teenager.

Goals are simply things that you want to achieve. They can be big or small, long-term or short-term.

The important thing is that you have a clear idea of what you want to achieve and are willing to put in the hard work to make it happen.

Not only will this help you to focus on what's important to you, but it will also give you a sense of purpose and direction.

Here are some tips to help you set goals:

1 **Think about what you want to achieve.** The first step is to sit down and think about what you want to achieve. This could be anything from getting good grades in school to becoming a professional athlete.

2 **Be specific.** Once you've thought about what you want to achieve, try to be as clear as possible. This will help you better focus on your goal and increase your chances of achieving it.

For example, rather than "getting good grades," you could set the goal of "getting an A in science."

3 **Be realistic.** Make sure that your goal is achievable. There's no point in setting a goal that's impossible to achieve. This doesn't mean that you should only set goals that are easy to achieve, but rather that you should set goals that are challenging but still within reach.

4 **Set a deadline.** If you can, try to set a deadline for your goal. This will help you stay on track and ensure you don't get sidetracked. Without a deadline, it's easy to put off working towards your goal until "someday."

5 **Write it down.** Once you've decided on your goal, write it down. This will help you better remember what you're trying to achieve and keep you accountable. You can also share your goal with someone else to help keep you accountable and on track.

Some people use the SMART goal method to narrow down what they want to achieve. **SMART stands for S-specific, M-measurable, A-attainable, R-relevant, and T-timely.**

SPECIFIC	MEASURABLE	ATTAINABLE	RELEVANT	TIMELY
What exactly do you want to achieve?	Establish clear measurements to track the achievement of your goal.	Outline the exact steps to achieve your goal.	Is your goal relevant to the strengths you possess? Is it relevant to your mission?	Do you have a time-frame to guide you in achieving your goal?

For example, let's say you want to get fit: "I will work out three times a week" is a great start, but it's not very specific.

A more specific goal would be "I will work out for thirty minutes, three times a week, at the gym."

This goal is much easier to achieve because it is more specific. So if we go through the SMART list with the same example.

S-specific: "I will work out for thirty minutes at the gym three times a week."

M-measurable: You can measure this goal by whether or not you actually go to the gym three times a week and work out for thirty minutes each time.

A-attainable: The goal is attainable because it is realistic to go to the gym three times a week.

R-relevant: This goal is relevant because going to the gym is a great way to get fit.

T-timely: This goal is timely because of the amount of time you will spend working out each week, and you can start working out this week.

Now that you know what the SMART goal method is, you can use it to set your own goals.

Have a think about a goal you want to achieve: it could be something related to school, your hobbies, or your future career.

Once you have decided on your goal, use the SMART goal method to make it more specific. Write down your goal and keep it somewhere you can see it often to help you stay on track.

Now that we've covered how to set goals, let's look at how to achieve them.

. . . .
HOW TO ACHIEVE GOALS

1 Break them down into smaller pieces
The best way to achieve your goals is to break them down into smaller, more manageable pieces.

This will make them seem less daunting and help you better focus on what you need to do.

For example, if your goal is to get an A in math, your first step might be attending all your math classes.

Your second step might be doing all the homework and practice problems. And your third step might be to get help from a tutor or teacher if you're struggling.

By breaking down your goal into smaller steps, you'll increase your chances of achieving it.

❷ Create a plan of action

Now that you've decided on your goal and have broken it down into smaller steps, it's time to create an action plan. **This is simply a list of what you need to do to achieve your goal.**

For each step, you'll want to include a specific action that you need to take.

For example, if your goal is to get an A in math, your plan of action might be:

— attend all math classes

— do all homework and practice problems

— get help from a tutor or teacher if needed

This is just a basic example, but it gives you an idea of how to create a plan of action.

Remember, the more specific your plan of action is, the better.

❸ Take action and stay motivated

Once you've created your action plan, it's time to start taking action. This is where the real work begins.

You'll need to stay focused and motivated to achieve your goal.

One way to do this is to set regular reminders and reward yourself for taking action towards your goal.

> *For example, you could give yourself a small treat after completing each action plan step.*
>
> *This could be watching an extra episode of your favorite TV show or going for a walk in the park.*

The important thing is to find something that motivates you and helps you stay on track.

❹ Celebrate your achievements

Well done, you've done it! You've hit your goal. This is an exciting moment!

Take time to celebrate your accomplishment.

Once you've celebrated, it's time to set a new goal. This will help you to continue growing and developing as a person.

Remember, goal setting is an important life skill that can help you achieve anything you want. So don't be afraid to set goals and go after them! You can do it.

HOW TO KEEP MOTIVATED AND STAY ON TRACK

Staying on track can be difficult, especially when dealing with teenage life pressures.

There will be times when you feel like giving up or feel like you're not good enough. That's why it's crucial to have a support network of friends and family who can encourage you to keep going.

Here are some other tips to help you stay motivated:

 Set yourself regular reminders. Write your goals down and put them somewhere you'll see them daily. This could be on your fridge, door, or phone.

 Find a role model. Look for someone who has already achieved what you want to achieve and use them as motivation to keep going. *For example, suppose your goal is to play football professionally. In that case, you might look up inspirational quotes or watch videos of other football players.*

3 **Talk to others about your goals.** Sharing your goals with others can help motivate you to stay on track. You might even find a friend who wants to achieve the same goals as you, and you can work together.

4 **Take time to rest and recharge when you need it.** Staying motivated and on track can be exhausting, so make sure you take time to relax and rejuvenate. This could mean working out, getting enough sleep each night, or simply spending some time alone doing something you enjoy.

HOW TO BE CONFIDENT

The pre-teenage years can be a tough time. You're dealing with hormonal changes, peer pressure, and the stress of school. It's no wonder that so many teenagers lack confidence.

But being confident is an important life skill you need to learn. It's essential for achieving your goals, standing up for yourself, and enjoying a happy teenage experience.

> **I'VE FAILED OVER AND OVER AGAIN IN MY LIFE. THAT'S WHY I SUCCEED.**
>
> MICHAEL JORDAN,
> BASKETBALL PLAYER

Building confidence takes time and effort, but it's so worth it. Believe in yourself and stay positive. YOU CAN DO IT!

Here are some tips to help you build self-confidence:

1. **Believe in yourself.** You are amazing! The first step to being confident is to believe in yourself. This means accepting yourself for who you are and not comparing yourself to others. You are uniquely you!

2. **Set achievable goals.** Confidence comes from hitting your dreams, so set achievable and challenging goals. *For example, if you want to improve at tennis, practice a few times each week until you see improvement.*

3. **Find confident role models.** Look for people with qualities you admire, such as strength or compassion. You can learn much from observing how they behave and interact with others.

4. **Take risks and step out of your comfort zone.** Confidence comes from pushing outside of your comfort zone and trying new things. So go ahead and take that art class, join the football team or start a club! What's the worst thing that could happen?

5. **Don't be afraid to fail.** Failing is part of life and how we learn and grow. So don't be scared to make mistakes—they're essential to becoming confident.

ACTIVITY

Goal Ladder Visualization

This simple goal-setting activity helps break down big goals into smaller steps.

1. **Write down your DREAM on the top rung of the ladder.** It can be anything, but try to be specific. For example, if you want to improve at football, write, "I want to make the school team."

2. **On the first rung, write down your first goal and what action you need to do to hit that goal.** This will be your first ACTION STEP! For example, "I will attend training sessions 3 times a week" or "I will eat a healthy breakfast every day."

3. Move on to the second rung and set a new goal and what action you will take to achieve it. This is your second ACTION STEP! For example, "I will do some extra training at home" or "I will make sure I get 8 hours of sleep every night."

4. **Keep going until you reach the top of the ladder** (your DREAM). You should now have a list of ACTION STEPS that you need to take to achieve your DREAM!

5. Tick them off as you go

GOAL LADDER

Write your DREAM at the top, and then write each action
& step you'll take to achieve your goal.

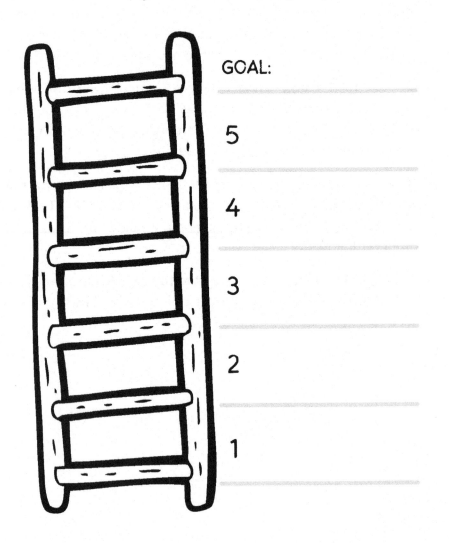

GOAL:

5

4

3

2

1

CHAPTER 2

FRIENDS & RELATIONSHIPS

> ◎ ◎ ◎ ◎ ◎ ◎ ◎ ◎ ◎ ◎ ◎ ◎ ◎ ◎ ◎ ◎ ◎
>
> FRIENDS ARE AN ESSENTIAL PART OF OUR LIVES. We rely on them for support and guidance as we grow and learn. The friends you make today will likely be with you for life.

This chapter will discuss what makes a good friend, how to make friends, and how to develop healthy relationships.

MAKING FRIENDS

What qualities do you look for in a friend?

Think about the friends you have now. What do you like about them?

Do you have any friends or relatives that you don't see very often, but it's like you never left each other's side when you are together?

These are the types of friends you want to have. They are the ones who make you feel good about yourself and make you laugh. They are supportive and understanding. They are the friends who will be there for you through thick and thin.

When looking for friends, think about the essential qualities to you. Do you want someone who is active and likes to go out and do things? Or do you want someone who is quieter and likes to stay home? We tend to find people who have similar interests. This can help you connect on a deeper level.

HOW TO MAKE FRIENDS

It can be tricky making friends when you're young. If you've joined a new school or moved to a new neighborhood, finding people with similar interests can be tricky. As the new kid, you may feel shy, or like you don't fit in. Just remember they were all new once, and you'll make friends in no time with a bit of effort.

Here are some tips on how to make friends:

 Join clubs or teams: This is a great way to meet people with similar interests outside school.

 Be yourself! You are amazing! You are uniquely you! Don't try to be someone you're not. People will like you for who you are.

 Put yourself out there. Talk to people. Smile. The more approachable you seem, the more likely people will talk to you.

 Be a good listener. Let the other person talk and be interested in what they say. Ask people about their day, their hobbies, or their interests. People love to talk about themselves. By showing an interest in others, they will be more likely to take an interest in you.

5 **Offer help when you can.** People will appreciate it, and it's a great way to make friends. If someone seems lost, offer to show them around the school or help them find their locker. If someone is having trouble with their homework, offer to help.

Remember, making friends takes time and effort. Don't get discouraged if you don't find your best friend overnight.

. . . .

HOW TO BE A GOOD FRIEND

When you're a good friend, you make the people around you feel good about themselves. You are supportive and understanding. You are there when things are tough, and you celebrate the good times together. You are someone that others can rely on.

Here are some tips on how to be a good friend:

1 **Be there for your friends when they need you.** Be there for them, whether they're having a bad day or having a tough time. Listen to them and offer help if you can.

2 **Be honest with your friends.** Don't try to hide things from them or lie to them. They will appreciate your honesty, and it will help build a stronger friendship.

3 **Be respectful of your friends.** Listen to what they have to say and don't judge them.

4 **Be positive.** Offer encouragement when your friends need it. Nobody likes a negative Nancy.

5 **Be a good listener.** Listen to them when your friends are talking and be interested in what they say. Let them finish their thoughts.

Always treat your friends with respect. Remember, they are essential people in your life, and you should cherish your friendship.

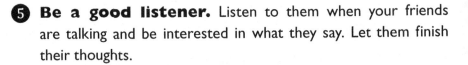

DEVELOPING HEALTHY RELATIONSHIPS

Although you may not seem ready yet. When you become a teenager, you may start dating or have a serious relationship.

However, not all relationships are healthy. **Healthy relationships, like friendships, are built on trust, respect, and communication.** If you're in a relationship that makes you feel bad about yourself, or if you are constantly fighting, that's not a healthy relationship.

Let's explore what makes a healthy relationship.

Trust

Trust is the foundation on which everything else is built. If you don't trust someone, having a healthy relationship with them will be tough.

What is trust? **Trust is being able to rely on someone.** Knowing that they will be there for you when you need them. Trust is being able to tell someone a secret and know that your secrets are safe with them.

In addition, you should always be honest with the other person. If you're not comfortable with something, tell them. Honesty is the best policy.

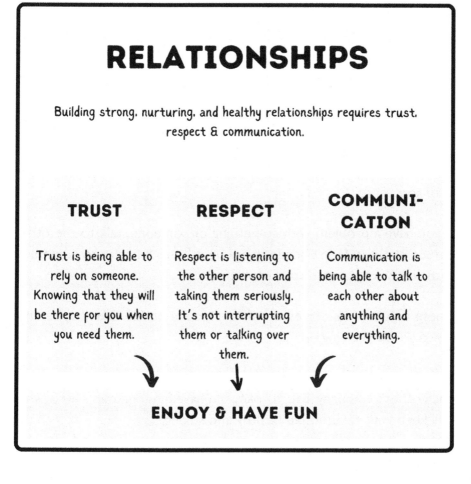

RELATIONSHIPS

Building strong, nurturing, and healthy relationships requires trust, respect & communication.

TRUST

Trust is being able to rely on someone. Knowing that they will be there for you when you need them.

RESPECT

Respect is listening to the other person and taking them seriously. It's not interrupting them or talking over them.

COMMUNI-CATION

Communication is being able to talk to each other about anything and everything.

ENJOY & HAVE FUN

Respect

Respect is essential in any relationship. You should respect the other person for who they are, and they should respect you in return. This includes respecting your opinions, your beliefs, and your boundaries. If there's no respect, there's no relationship.

What is respect? **Respect is listening to the other person and taking them seriously.** It's not interrupting them or talking over them. If you respect someone, you can agree to disagree. You recognize the other person has a right to their own opinion, even if you disagree with it.

Communication

Communication is vital in any relationship. **You need to be able to talk to each other about anything and everything.** It will not be a healthy relationship if you're not comfortable communicating with someone.

If you have a problem with something or someone, talk to the other person about it. Don't bottle things up. It's much better to communicate and work through your problems.

These three things are essential in any relationship, but they're vital when you're growing up.

Finally, remember to have fun! Relationships are all about enjoying each other's company. Laugh, joke, and have fun together. This is what will keep your relationship healthy and strong.

BULLYING

Bullying is a problem that many kids face. It can be tough being bullied, and it can be hard to know what to do. It can make you feel scared, alone, and helpless.

Bullying is when someone repeatedly and purposely says or does mean things to hurt another person. It's not a one-time thing; it's something that happens over and over again.

Bullying comes in many different forms. It can be physical (hitting, kicking), verbal (calling names, making threats), or social (leaving someone out, spreading rumors). It can also happen online, through text messages or social media.

No matter what type of bullying someone uses, it's NEVER okay.

But there are ways that you can deal with bullying and get help.

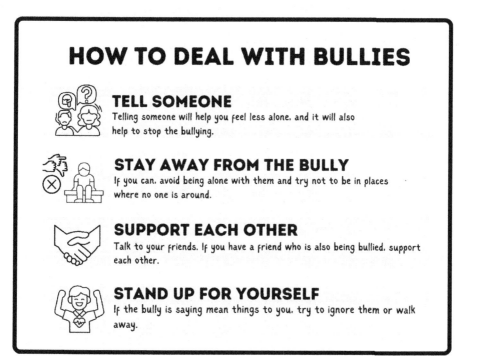

HOW TO DEAL WITH BULLIES

TELL SOMEONE
Telling someone will help you feel less alone, and it will also help to stop the bullying.

STAY AWAY FROM THE BULLY
If you can, avoid being alone with them and try not to be in places where no one is around.

SUPPORT EACH OTHER
Talk to your friends. If you have a friend who is also being bullied, support each other.

STAND UP FOR YOURSELF
If the bully is saying mean things to you, try to ignore them or walk away.

How to deal with bullies

- **Tell someone.** Talk to a parent, teacher, or friend. Telling someone will help you feel less alone, and it will also help to stop the bullying. You may worry that you're being a tattletale by telling someone, but that's not true. Telling someone about bullying is vital so that it can be stopped.

- **Stay away from the bully.** If you can, avoid being alone with them and try not to be in places where no one is around. This can be hard if the bully is someone you see at school every day, but it's essential to do what you can to stay safe.

- **Support each other.** If you have a friend who is also being bullied, support each other. You can talk to each other about how you're feeling and help each other stay strong.

- **Stand up for yourself.** This can be hard, but it's essential to do what you can to stop the bullying. If the bully is saying mean things to you, try to ignore them or walk away. Tell them to stop and try to get away from them if they hit you.

Dealing with bullying can be challenging, but you don't have to face it alone. There are people who can help, and there are ways that you can deal with the bully. Remember to stay strong and not let them get the best of you. BULLIES NEVER WIN IN THE END.

CYBERBULLYING

Cyberbullying is a different type of bullying over the internet or through electronic devices. **Cyberbullying can include sending mean text messages, posting hurtful comments, or sharing photos on social media sites.**

Kids who are cyberbullied can feel scared, alone, and helpless. If you're being cyberbullied, it's important to remember that you're not alone. There are people who care about you and want to help.

There are a few things you can do to try to stop cyberbullying:

- **Tell a trusted adult about what's going on.** They can help you figure out the best way to deal with the situation. If a classmate or school friend is doing the bullying, talk to your teacher about it.

- **Block the person who is bullying you.** This will make it harder for them to contact you and may stop the bullying.

- **Keep your social media accounts private.** Don't share personal information or photos that could be used to hurt you.

- **Don't respond to the bully.** This can just encourage them and make the situation worse. Walking away and ignoring the bully, however hard, is always the best course of action.

- **Save any evidence of the bullying (texts, emails, photos, etc.).** This can help prove what's happening if you need to report it.

- **Contact the social media site.** Most sites have policies against cyberbullying and will take steps to remove malicious content if it's reported.

With the rise of social media, cyberbullying has become a growing problem. Bullying is never okay. If you're being cyberbullied, don't suffer in silence. Remember, you're not alone. Tell a trusted adult immediately. They can help you figure out the best way to deal with the situation.

GOSSIP

Gossip is another form of bullying.

It involves spreading rumors, secrets, or hurtful things about another person. It can be spread by word of mouth or through social media, text messages, or email.

Gossip can be just as hurtful as saying something to someone's face. It can damage relationships. When you're the subject of gossip, it can be hard to know who to trust and feel like everyone is talking about you behind your back. You may feel alone and like nobody understands what you're going through.

But there are ways that you can deal with gossip.

How to deal with gossip

- **Talk to a trusted adult about what's going on.** This can be a parent, teacher, or counselor. They can help you figure out what to do next.

- **Ignore the gossip.** This can be hard to do, but it's important to remember that what people say is not necessarily true. People gossip because they want to make themselves feel better, not because they care about you.

- **Stand up for yourself.** Talk to the person who is spreading the rumor. Ask them to stop. If people say mean things about you, don't be afraid to speak up and tell them that it's not okay.

- **Stay away from gossips.** If someone is constantly starting rumors or spreading gossip, it's best to stay away from them.
  There's no reason to put yourself in a situation where you will feel
  uncomfortable or upset.

Being on the receiving end of gossip can be rough, but remember, it's
not about you. People gossip because they want to make themselves
feel more important and popular.

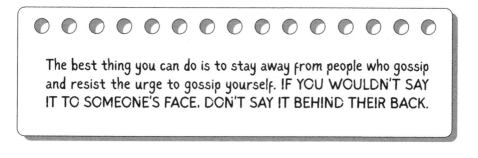

The best thing you can do is to stay away from people who gossip
and resist the urge to gossip yourself. IF YOU WOULDN'T SAY
IT TO SOMEONE'S FACE, DON'T SAY IT BEHIND THEIR BACK.

ACTIVITY

Friendship & Healthy Relationship Rules

Write down some friendship rules that you think are important. Here are some examples to get you started:

- Be honest with your friends.
- Be there for your friends when they need you.
- Listen to your friends and be interested in what they say.
- Offer help and encouragement when your friends need it.

FRIENDSHIP

WHAT ARE SOME FRIENDSHIP RULES THAT YOU HAVE?
WRITE DOWN SOME THINGS THAT ARE IMPORTANT TO YOU:

1 _____

2 _____

3 _____

4 _____

5 _____

6 _____

7 _____

8 _____

9 _____

10 _____

CHAPTER 3

EMOTIONS

As you grow older, you will be experiencing lots of new things, some good and some bad. You might find yourself feeling happy one minute and sad the next. It's important to take care of yourself during this time, both physically and emotionally. In this chapter, we will discuss some ways to do just that.

What are emotions?

Emotions are feelings that we experience in response to different situations. They can be positive, such as happiness or love, or negative, like sadness or anger. Emotions can be powerful and affect our behavior, thoughts, and physical health.

Knowing how to deal with these emotions in healthy ways is essential.

When it comes to positive emotions, enjoy them! Positive emotions can make us feel good both physically and mentally. They can also help us perform better at school or work. So don't be afraid to let yourself feel happy, loved, or excited.

. . . .

ANGER

Anger is a normal emotion but can become a problem if not managed correctly. When you are angry, your heart rate and blood pressure increase, your muscles tense up, and you might even feel like you could hurt someone.

It is natural to feel angry, but it is helpful to find healthy ways to deal with anger before it gets out of control.

HOW TO DEAL WITH ANGER

1 THINK ABOUT WHY YOU'RE ANGRY.

2 TAKE A DEEP BREATH AND COUNT TO 10

3 TAKE YOURSELF AWAY FROM THE SITUATION

4 TALK TO SOMEONE

5 EXERCISE AND 'SWEAT IT OUT'

6 DO SOMETHING CREATIVE

How to deal with anger

Some ways to deal with anger are:

- **Think about why you're angry.** Sometimes figuring out what is making you angry can help you deal with the feeling. Maybe there is something that you can do to change the situation, or perhaps you need to talk to someone about how you're feeling.

- **Take a deep breath and slowly count to 10.** This will help calm you down and give you time to think about what you want to do. Sometimes, slowing down and focusing on your breath can be enough to calm you down. Try taking in a deep breath through your nose and exhaling slowly through your mouth. Count to 10, and repeat. Let your shoulders relax as you do this.

- **Leave the situation that is making you angry.** If you are in a situation making you mad, such as an argument with your parents or a fight with your friends, it might be best to walk away. This will help you avoid saying or doing something you might regret later.

- **Talk to someone you trust about how you're feeling.** This can help you get rid of the anger by talking about it. It can also help you feel better because you are not keeping your feelings bottled up. Your Mom and Dad are a great place to start, but you can also talk to a friend, teacher, or counselor.

- **Do something physical to release the anger.** This could be anything from punching a pillow to going for a run. Physical activity can help release the anger and frustration you might feel and can be a good way of taking you out of the situation.

- **Think about how the situation might have been handled differently.** This can help you learn from the experience and not feel as angry about it. You may find it helpful to write down what you are mad about. This can help you get your thoughts out. Seeing them on paper can also help you make sense of them.

- **Do something creative.** Drawing, painting, cooking, or building something can help you healthily express your anger. It can also help you calm down and focus on something else.

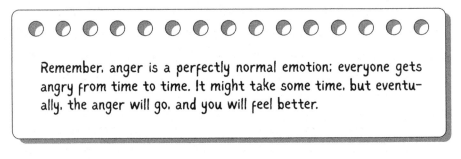

Remember, anger is a perfectly normal emotion; everyone gets angry from time to time. It might take some time, but eventually, the anger will go, and you will feel better.

The key is to find healthy ways to deal with it.

SADNESS

When we experience sadness, getting out of bed, eating, or even smiling can be challenging. We might feel like we are all alone in the world and that nobody understands what we are going through. We might want to hide away.

But sadness is a normal emotion, and it is okay to feel this way.

There are a lot of ways to deal with sadness. Some people might want to talk about their feelings, while others might prefer to keep to themselves.

How to deal with sadness

Some ways to deal with sadness are:

- **Talk to someone you trust about how you're feeling.** This can help you get rid of the sadness by talking about it. It can also help you feel better because you are sharing your feelings.

- **Write about your sadness.** This can be a journal entry or even a letter to yourself. Writing about your feelings can help you understand them better and make them more manageable.

- **Listen to music that makes you feel happy.** Music is a great way to boost your mood and help you forget about your sadness for a little while.

- **Get moving.** Exercise releases endorphins, which are chemicals that improve your mood. So go for a walk, run, or dance around your house to eliminate the sadness.

Remember, it is okay to feel sad sometimes. These tips can help you deal with those feelings and start to feel better.

FEAR

Fear is a natural emotion that is designed to protect us from danger. Everyone experiences it at some point in their life.

There are many reasons why we might feel fearful. We might be afraid of the dark, heights, or animals. We might be scared of something that we know is dangerous or fearful of something new or unfamiliar. It's perfectly natural to feel fear.

> Fear can help us protect ourselves from danger. It can also motivate us to do something we might not have done before, like overcoming our fears of speaking in public. OVERCOMING FEAR CAN GIVE US A SENSE OF ACCOMPLISHMENT AND MAKE US FEEL MORE CONFIDENT. IT CAN HELP US GROW.

However, fear can become a problem when it starts interfering with our everyday lives. For example, suppose you are afraid of flying. In that case, this might prevent you from going on holiday or visiting family and friends who live far away. If we are constantly avoiding things that make us afraid, this can hurt our lives.

Sometimes we can feel fear when there is no danger, or the threat is less significant than the fear. This can be really scary, and it can stop us from doing things we want to do.

How to overcome fear

There are many ways to deal with fear. Some people might want to face their fears head-on, while others prefer a more gradual approach.

Some ways to deal with fear are:

- **Talk to someone about your fears.** This can help you understand them better and start to work on overcoming them.

- **Write down your fears.** This can help you see them differently and start to work through them.

- **Expose yourself to the things that scare you bit by bit.** This can be very effective in overcoming fear. However, doing this gradually and with someone you trust is essential.

- **Relax.** Relaxation techniques can help you deal with the physical symptoms of fear, such as increased heart rate and sweating.

Remember, you are not alone. Everyone experiences fear. It is a natural emotion that can be helpful to us. But if fear starts to interfere with our lives, there are things we can do to deal with it.

STRESS AND ANXIETY

Anxiety and stress are two of the most common emotions that people experience. They can both be very unpleasant.

Anxiety is caused by worry and fear. It can be caused by events that have already happened or things that might happen in the future. Sometimes we worry about things that are very unlikely to happen.

Stress is the physical response to anxiety. It can cause problems like headaches, upset stomachs, and difficulty sleeping.

Many things can cause stress. At school, you might feel stressed about homework or exams. Or with your friends, you might feel stressed about who will be at a party. It's perfectly normal to feel stressed sometimes.

How to deal with stress and anxiety

While there are many different ways to deal with stress and anxiety, some basic tips can help you get started.

BASIC TIPS TO HELP DEAL WITH
STRESS AND ANXIETY

1 TRY TO UNDERSTAND WHAT IS CAUSING YOUR STRESS AND ANXIETY. — This can be difficult, but once you identify the cause, you can begin to work on addressing it. If you are unsure what is causing your stress or anxiety, many resources can help you figure it out.

2 TRY TO MANAGE YOUR STRESS AND ANXIETY — This means taking care of yourself both physically and emotionally. Make sure you get enough sleep, eat a healthy diet, and exercise regularly. Taking some time for yourself each day can also help reduce your stress and anxiety.

3 AVOID THINGS THAT TRIGGERS YOUR STRESS AND ANXIETY — This might mean avoiding certain people or situations. If you can't avoid the trigger, try to change how you think about it. For example, if you're anxious about an upcoming test, tell yourself that you are prepared and can do it.

First, **try to understand what is causing your stress and anxiety**. This can be difficult, but once you identify the cause, you can begin to work on addressing it. If you are unsure what is causing your stress or anxiety, many resources can help you figure it out.

Second, it is vital to **manage your stress and anxiety**. This means taking care of yourself both physically and emotionally. Make sure you get enough sleep, eat a healthy diet, and exercise regularly. Taking some time for yourself each day can also help reduce your stress and anxiety.

Finally, try to **avoid things that trigger your stress and anxiety**. This might mean avoiding certain people or situations. If you can't avoid the trigger, try to change how you think about it. For example, if you're anxious about an upcoming test, tell yourself that you are prepared and can do it.

Remember, everyone experiences stress and anxiety in different ways. What works for one person might not work for another. If you don't find the answers you are looking for, **consult a mental health professional**. They can help you find the best way to deal with stress and anxiety.

ACTIVITY

Stress & Anxiety Action Plan

This is a simple activity, but it can be very helpful in understanding what may be causing your stress and anxiety and working out ways to deal with it.

1. In the first column, write down things that cause you stress or anxiety. Try to put them in order, with the things that cause you most stress at the top; for example, you may include:
   - Taking tests
   - Being around people I don't know well

2. In the following column, for each of the things you wrote down, brainstorm at least two ways to deal with the stress or anxiety it causes. For example:
   - Taking tests:
     - Study ahead of time
     - Take breaks during the test
   - Being around people I don't know well:
     - Talk to someone you do know before going into the situation
     - Bring a friend with you

3. Write down when you will complete it in the last column.

STRESS
ACTION PLAN

What's stressing me out?	What I can do about it?	When can I do it?

CHAPTER 4

SCHOOL AND LEARNING

Going to school is an important part of growing up. It's a place where you learn about the world around you, make friends and develop life skills. But for some kids, starting school or moving to a new school can be a bit scary. If you're feeling nervous about starting school, don't worry!

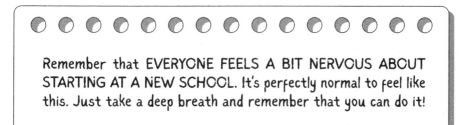

Remember that EVERYONE FEELS A BIT NERVOUS ABOUT STARTING AT A NEW SCHOOL. It's perfectly normal to feel like this. Just take a deep breath and remember that you can do it!

Remember too; there are many great things about going to school, like learning new things and meeting new friends. Of course, one of the most important things about school is that it teaches you how to learn and work hard. These skills will serve you well throughout your life. No matter what you do, always give it your best effort and never give up!

Try to listen to your teachers and do your best at school. This is the best way to learn and get good grades.

But it's also important to be yourself. Don't try to be someone you're not because you'll only end up feeling unhappy.

The most important thing is to have fun and enjoy your time at school. It's a place where you learn new things and make lasting friendships. So go out there and have some fun!

Of course, you'll also have to take regular exams and tests at school. This can be daunting, but remember that everyone gets nervous about these things. Just do your best, and you'll be fine.

GETTING GOOD GRADES AT SCHOOL

Getting good grades at school will help set you up for life. But it can be hard to know where to start. If you're struggling to get good grades, don't worry! We've got some great tips to help you out.

 The first step is to make sure you understand the material. Ask your teacher or a friend if you're unsure about something. The more you know, the easier it will be to do well on tests and exams.

2 **Another critical step is to stay organized.** Keep track of due dates and ensure you have all the materials you need for each class. This will help you stay on top of your work and hand things in on time.

3 **Try to study regularly.** Dedicate some time each day or each week to reviewing the material. This will help you remember things better and get good grades.

④ Finally, don't stress out! Getting good grades is important, but it's not worth getting stressed out about. Take a deep breath and do your best. You'll be fine!

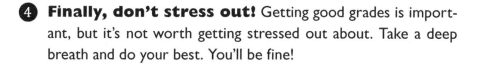

HOW TO STUDY EFFECTIVELY

You need to study effectively if you want to do well in school. But what does that mean? And how can you do it? Here are some tips:

① Start by making a study plan. Decide which subjects you need to focus on and devise a study schedule. This will help you stay organized and make the most of your time.

② Make sure you have enough space to study. You need to be comfortable when you're learning, so find a quiet place where you can concentrate.

③ Create a study environment that works for you. Some people like to listen to music or have complete silence when they study, while others prefer to be around people. Find what works best for you and stick to it.

④ Take breaks. Try to take breaks when studying, especially if you've been working for a while. Get up and walk around, or have a snack. This will help you stay focused and motivated.

DEALING WITH HOMEWORK

As you grow older, you're likely to be set homework. At first, this can be challenging. You may feel like you don't have enough time or are always behind. But don't worry, with a little organization, it's manageable. Here are some tips to help you out.

1. **Make a schedule and stick to it.** Decide how much time you need for each subject and stick to that schedule. This will help you stay organized and avoid last-minute cramming.

2. **Get organized.** Keep track of your homework assignments and due dates. Don't bury your head in the sand! Try to stay on top of things and hand assignments in on time.

3. **Ask for help when you need it.** If you're struggling with a particular subject, don't hesitate to ask your teacher or a friend for help. They'll be happy to assist you.

4. **Take breaks.** Remember to take breaks when doing homework, especially if you've been working for a while. Get up and walk around, or have a snack. This will help you stay focused and motivated.

5. **Stay positive.** When you're doing homework, it's easy to get frustrated. But remember that everyone makes mistakes. Don't get discouraged, and keep trying your best.

6. **Practice, practice, practice.** The best way to improve your grades is to practice. If you can, try solving sample questions or practicing past exams. This will help you become more familiar with the material and do better on tests.

HOW TO ACE TESTS

One of the skills you will learn in school is how to take tests. If you've never taken an exam before, it can be daunting. Tests are usually timed, and you can't bring anything with you into the room. You may feel under pressure like you're in a race against the clock. But like anything, practice makes perfect!

7 TIPS ON HOW TO ACE TESTS

RELAX

The first thing you need to do is relax. You're more likely to do well if you're calm and focused. So take a few deep breaths, clear your head, and get ready to tackle the test.

TIME YOURSELF

When taking a test, you want to ensure you have enough time for each question. So before you start, decide how much time you want to spend on each section. This will help you stay on track and not run out of time.

READ THE QUESTIONS CAREFULLY

Don't rush through the test. Stop, pause and read each question carefully. This will help you understand what is being asked and ensure you answer the question correctly.

ANSWER THE EASY QUESTIONS FIRST

If you're struggling with a question, try answering the more straightforward questions first. This will give you a better idea of how much time you have left for the more complex questions.

CHECK YOUR WORK

Once you've finished, go back and check your work. Make sure you answered all the questions and that your answers are correct.

TAKE A BREAK

Once you've finished the test, take a break. Get up and walk around, or have a snack. This will help you calm down and clear your head.

DON'T WORRY

If you don't do well on a test, don't worry. It's not the end of the world! Some people do well at tests, while others find them difficult. Tests are just one part of the assessment process. There are other ways to show your knowledge and understanding.

HOW TO REMEMBER INFORMATION

Remembering information is an essential life skill. When you're in school, you will be required to retain a lot of facts. You'll also meet many new people, and it's good to remember their names. If you can place a person's name, you're more likely to make a good impression on them. And if you remember important facts, you're more likely to do well in your studies.

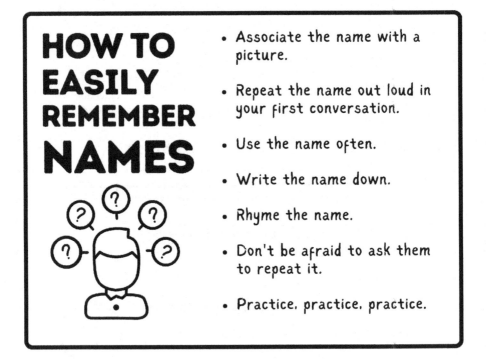

HOW TO EASILY REMEMBER NAMES

- Associate the name with a picture.

- Repeat the name out loud in your first conversation.

- Use the name often.

- Write the name down.

- Rhyme the name.

- Don't be afraid to ask them to repeat it.

- Practice, practice, practice.

You may think you're not good at remembering things, but everyone can improve their memory if they practice regularly. **The brain is a muscle. The more you use it, the stronger it will get.**

Here are some tips to help you remember names, which could also be used to remember facts.

1 **Associate the name with a picture.** The human brain is excellent at remembering images. So when you meet someone new, try associating their name with a picture in your head. This will help you remember it better. You could create a funny or silly image as you may remember it better that way.

2 **Repeat the name out loud in your first conversation.** Repeating the word aloud will help you internalize and remember it better. For example, if you're introduced to someone called Angie, instead of saying "nice to meet you," say "Hi Angie, it's nice to meet you."

3 **Use the name often.** When you use someone's name regularly, you're more likely to remember it. So try using the person's name in every conversation you have with them. Not only will this help you remember it better, but it will also make the person feel important and special.

4 **Write the name down.** When you meet someone, take a few seconds to write their name down. You could put the person's name in your phone contacts or write it on a piece of paper. You could take it further by connecting them with an important fact you've learned about them. For example, if you meet someone called Sarah, you could write "Sarah loves singing" next to her name.

5 **Rhyme the name.** This is a great way to remember someone's name if you're having trouble doing so. Try to think of a rhyme with their name when you meet someone. For example, if someone's name is Anna, you could rhyme it with "banana."

6 **Don't be afraid to ask them to repeat it.** It's okay to make mistakes when trying to remember someone's name. If you forget their name, don't be afraid to ask them to repeat it. And if you still can't remember it, don't worry about it. Just move on and try to remember the person's name the next time you see them.

7 **Practice, practice, practice.** The best way to remember something is to practice. If you can, try repeating the name a few times. This will help embed it in your memory.

The same is valid for remembering facts. If you want to remember something, you need to practice regularly. Some people find it helpful to write the information down, while others prefer to recite it aloud. If you can find a way to make the information exciting or fun, you're more likely to remember it.

Practicing these tips regularly is essential so that they become second nature to you. The more you practice, the better your memory will be. Good luck!

ACTIVITY

Homework Planner

Use the simple homework planner to plan your next assignments.

	Subject	To-do	Due date
☐			
☐			
☐			
☐			
☐			
☐			
☐			

CHAPTER 5

HEALTH AND WELLNESS

Health and wellness are essential aspects of life that we should all strive to maintain. They aren't just about being physically healthy, but also mentally and emotionally healthy.

When it comes to health and wellness, there are a few key things everyone should know and practice.

This chapter will discuss some of the most essential health and wellness topics. We will discuss the importance of eating healthy, staying active, and getting enough sleep.

EXERCISE

One of the most important aspects of good health is staying physically active.

EXERCISE IS CRUCIAL FOR OVERALL HEALTH AND WELL-BEING, and it's especially important during your pre-teen years.

Exercise helps build muscle, improve strength and endurance, and burn calories. It also releases endorphins, which are chemicals in the brain that have mood-boosting effects. In other words, exercise can help improve your mood and reduce stress.

How to exercise more

There are many different ways to stay active and get exercise. You can join a sports team, go for walks or runs, or even play in your backyard. The important thing is to find something that you enjoy and to do it regularly.

If you don't like running, there's no point in forcing yourself to do it. But, it's also good to challenge yourself and push yourself outside of your comfort zone from time to time. This will help you to become stronger and more resilient.

Try to do at least 30 minutes of exercise each day. This doesn't have to be all at once—you can break it up into 10-minute intervals if that's easier for you.

You could:

- Ride your bike or scooter
- Walk to school
- Jump on a trampoline
- Swim
- Play tag with your friends
- Do some pushups or sit-ups
- Run around the block
- Do a simple workout

Try to incorporate your exercise into your daily routine so that it becomes a habit. For example, if you usually watch TV after school for an hour, try doing a 20-minute workout and then watching TV for the remaining 40 minutes.

Alternatively, you could incorporate exercise into your school day, so instead of driving to school, walk or ride your bike.

HEALTHY EATING

Another aspect of good health is eating a balanced and healthy diet. **Eating healthy foods helps our bodies to function correctly and to stay strong.** It also helps us maintain a healthy weight, which is important for our physical and mental health.

A balanced diet includes foods from all the major food groups: fruits, vegetables, grains, dairy, and protein. It's important to eat a variety of different foods from each group so that we get all the nutrients our bodies need.

How to eat healthily

We have covered the need for a balanced diet above, but how do you actually put this into practice?

There are a few simple tips that can help you to make healthier choices:

1 **Eat a healthy breakfast every day:** Breakfast is the day's most important meal. It helps jumpstart your metabolism and give you energy for the day ahead.

2 **Make half your plate fruits and vegetables:** Fruits and vegetables are packed with nutrients essential for good health. Try to include a variety of different colors and types to get a variety of nutrients. You should aim for at least 5 servings of fruit and vegetables every day.

3 **Avoid processed foods:** Processed foods (such as chips, cookies, cakes, and ice cream) are often high in sugar, salt, and unhealthy fats and low in nutrients. Try to eat less of these foods and instead focus on eating whole, unprocessed foods (such as fruits, vegetables, whole grains, and lean protein).

4 **Limit sugary drinks:** Sugary drinks are often high in sugar and provide very little nutritional value. Instead of sugary drinks, try to drink water, milk, or 100% fruit juice.

5 **Enjoy everything in moderation:** It's okay to enjoy your favorite foods from time to time. Just remember to eat them in moderation (small amounts) and balance them with healthier choices.

6 **Be active:** As we mentioned, exercise is vital for good health. Try to be active for at least 30 minutes each day.

7 **Drink plenty of water:** Water is essential for our bodies to function properly. It helps to transport nutrients and to keep our cells hydrated. Try to drink 8 glasses of water each day.

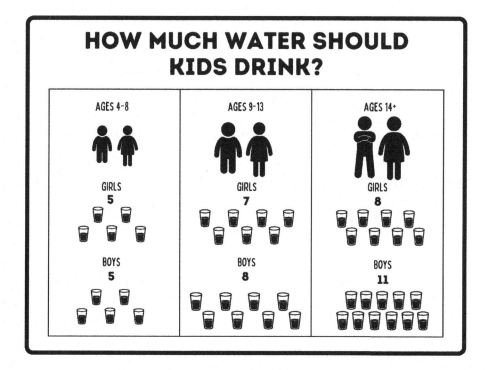

There are many aspects of good health, but eating a balanced diet and regular exercise will help your body function properly and stay strong. Try to incorporate healthy eating and exercise into your daily routine so that they become habits. These habits will help you to stay healthy throughout your life.

HOW TO ENSURE YOU GET ENOUGH SLEEP

Getting enough sleep is another part of good health. **During sleep, our bodies rest, recharge and rebuild tissues, muscles, and bone.**

A good night's sleep usually means around 8 hours of uninterrupted sleep for adults and 10 hours or more for children. If you don't get enough sleep, you may feel tired during the day, have trouble concentrating, and you may be more likely to get sick and feel stressed out. **Sleep is quite literally your superpower!**

There are a few things you can do to help improve the quality of your sleep:

 Establish a regular sleep schedule and stick to it as much as possible. This means going to bed at the same time each night and getting up at the same time each morning, even on weekends.

 Create a bedtime routine to help you relax before sleep. This could involve things like reading or taking a bath.

3 **Avoid screens (TV, phones, laptops) in the hour leading up to bedtime** as the blue light from screens can make it harder to fall asleep. It's a good idea to switch off all electronic devices in your bedroom or remove them from the room altogether.

4 **Create a calm and inviting environment in your bedroom.** This means making sure it's dark, quiet, and cool. Your bedroom should be a place where you feel relaxed and comfortable.

⑤ Get regular exercise during the day. Exercise helps to promote good sleep. It helps tire out your body and releases endorphins, which can help you to relax and fall asleep more easily.

Tips to recharge your superpower!

Create a relaxing
evening routine
every night

Go to bed
at the same time
each night

Read a
book

Take a
relaxing bath

Avoid screens in
the hour before
bedtime

Ensure you get
enough fresh air,
sunlight, & exercise
during the day.

Create a calm
environment in your
bedroom – dark,
quiet & cool

THE IMPORTANCE OF GOOD HYGIENE

Another aspect of good health is keeping our bodies clean. This means washing your hands regularly, brushing your teeth twice a day, and showering or bathing.

Throughout the day, our hands come into contact with many different surfaces, and they can pick up bacteria and other germs. If we don't wash our hands, we can spread these germs to other people or onto surfaces. This can lead to illnesses such as colds, flu, and stomach bugs.

HOW TO WASH YOUR HANDS

1 WET YOUR HANDS

2 APPLY SOME SOAP

3 RUB YOUR HANDS & CLEAN IN BETWEEN THE FINGERS

4 RINSE WITH WATER

5 DRY YOUR HANDS

When you should wash your hands:

- before, during, and after preparing food
- before eating food
- after using the restroom
- after coughing, sneezing, or blowing your nose
- after handling animals or animal waste
- after handling garbage

How to wash your hands

To wash your hands properly, use warm water and soap and scrub all over your hands for at least 20 seconds. Be sure to get in between your fingers and under your nails. Rinse well and dry with a clean towel.

How to brush your teeth

Brushing your teeth twice a day helps keep them healthy. Brushing removes plaque—a sticky film of bacteria—from your teeth. If plaque isn't removed, it can harden and turn into tartar, leading to gum disease.

To brush your teeth properly, **use a pea-sized amount of toothpaste on your toothbrush.** Aim the toothbrush at a 45-degree angle towards the gum line and use gentle circular motions. Be sure to brush on the inside surfaces of your teeth and use a light back and forth action on the chewing surfaces of your molars. Spit the toothpaste out after brushing.

Lastly, showering or bathing will help keep your skin clean and healthy. Use a mild soap or body wash and avoid scrubbing your skin too hard. Rinse the soap off, and then dry yourself with a clean towel.

Body smells and puberty

As you grow older, you might notice your start to smell different. This is perfectly normal! As your body goes through puberty, you might sweat more, and your skin will produce more oil. This can lead to body odor.

Puberty usually occurs between 10 and 14 for girls and between 12 and 16 for boys.

There are a few things you can do to help reduce body odor:

- Firstly, **shower or bathe every day.** This will help to remove sweat and bacteria from your skin.

- Secondly, **wear clean clothes.** You should wash your clothes regularly, especially items like socks and underwear.

- Thirdly, **use an antiperspirant or deodorant.** These products can help to mask body odor.

- Fourthly, **eat a healthy diet.** Eating foods that contain lots of fiber can help reduce body odor as they help flush toxins out of your body.

- Lastly, **drink plenty of water.** Staying hydrated will help to keep your skin healthy and free from bacteria.

ACTIVITY

Exercise Log

Regular exercise is essential for good health. It can help to improve your mood, reduce stress, and boost your energy levels.

Over the next week, keep track of your daily exercise. This could be going for a walk, a bike ride, or a swim. It could also be playing football, basketball, or soccer.

You can also include other activities that make you move, such as dancing, skipping, and running.

At the end of the week, add up all the minutes you exercised for each day. Then calculate the total number of minutes you exercised over the week.

How much exercise did you do this week?

Did you do more or less exercise than you thought you would?

How do you feel after completing this activity?

EXERCISE LOG

FILL OUT EACH DAY WITH YOUR DAILY EXERCISE. AT THE END OF THE WEEK, ADD UP ALL THE MINUTES YOU EXERCISED.

MONDAY

Activity: ☐

Minutes _____

TUESDAY

Activity: ☐

Minutes _____

WEDNESDAY

Activity: ☐

Minutes _____

THURSDAY

Activity: ☐

Minutes _____

FRIDAY

Activity: ☐

Minutes _____

SATURDAY / SUNDAY

Activity: ☐

Minutes _____

○ ○ ○ ○ ○ ○
m t w t f s s

Total
Minutes _____

CHAPTER 6

MONEY MATTERS

One of the most important things you will learn in this book is how to handle money. It is helpful to start learning about money as early as possible to make the most of it and be responsible with your finances when you are older.

There are a few things you need to know about money.

- **Firstly, you need to know how to earn it.** Money doesn't grow on trees—it comes from working hard. When you're young, this usually comes from doing chores around the house or getting an allowance from your parents. As you get older, you may start to earn money from part-time jobs.

- **Secondly, you need to know how to save it.** Let's say you have your eye on a new bike that costs $200. You can either save up for it over time or borrow the money from your parents (or someone else) and pay them back over time.

- **Thirdly, you need to know how to spend it.** Just because you have money doesn't mean you should go out and spend it all! You need to be mindful of what you are spending your money on and whether or not it is something you need. You might feel you need a new PlayStation 4 straight away, but is that a need? Or are you just wanting it because all your friends have one?

Learning about money is an important life skill, and it is something that will benefit you for the rest of your life. The more you know about money, the better off you will be financially.

Before we get started, let's look at some money-related words.

- CASH: This is paper money or the coins you have in your wallet or piggy bank.

- INCOME: This is the money that you earn. For example, if you receive a $50 per month allowance from your parents, that is your income.

- EXPENSES: This is the opposite of income — it is the money we spend on things. For example, if you spend $10 on a new toy, that is an expense.

- BUDGET: This is a plan that helps us track our income and expenses to save money.

- SAVING IS WHEN YOU PUT SOME OF YOUR MONEY ASIDE FOR LATER.

- INVESTING: This is when you use your money to make more!

- DEBT: This is when you owe somebody money.

Now that we have examined money-related words, let's dig deeper and learn more about these topics.

HOW TO BUDGET YOUR MONEY

Budgeting is an important life skill to learn. **It is planning for your future spending.** This means looking at your income and working out how much you need to save each month and what you can afford to spend.

> *For example, let's say you are saving for a new pair of jeans that cost $100. You will need to work out how much money you have coming in each month and how much you can afford to put away each month until you have enough for the jeans.*

When you start earning money, you may find that you spend it each month as you get it. But even if you put a small amount of money away, it's a good idea to start saving some each month to have money for later. You never know when you might need it!

If you can start a habit of saving when you're younger, it will become easier to save when you're older and earn more money.

HOW TO SAVE MONEY

One popular method for learning to save is the jar system. This is where you have different jars for different savings goals.

THE JAR SAVING METHOD

This is a popular method for learning to save. This is where you divide your money into different jars for different savings goals.

NEW JEANS

TRIP TO DISNEY LAND

NEW PET

For example, you might have a "new jeans" jar and a "new pet" jar.

You divide it every time you get money and put it into your different jars. This can be a fun way to save, and it also helps you see how much you are saving for each goal.

As you grow older, you may want to adopt another popular method: the 50/30/20 rule. In this case, you divide your money into three categories — **50% for essential expenses, 30% for things you really want, and 20% for savings.**

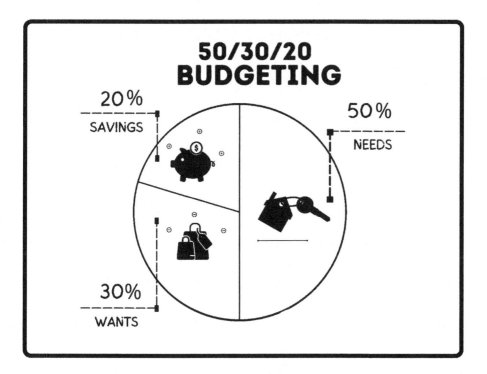

For example, if you received $100 birthday money, you would divide it up like this:

— $50 for essentials — this could be clothes or food

— $30 for wants — this could be a new toy or game

- $20 for savings—this could be put into your piggy bank or a savings account

The 50/30/20 rule is a good starting point, but you may need to adjust it depending on your income and expenses.

There are many ways to budget, and finding a system that works for you is vital. The most important thing is to be mindful of your spending and try to put some money away each month.

HOW TO SPEND MONEY WISELY

Now that you have a good idea about budgeting and how to save money, let's talk about spending money wisely.

When you choose to spend your money, think about whether you are buying something you need or if it is something you just want.

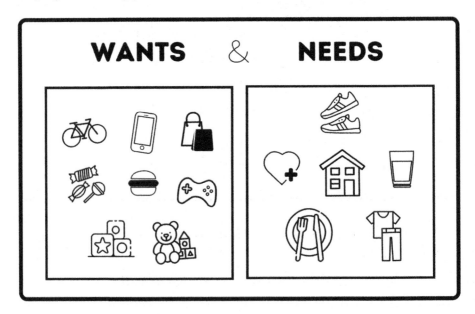

- **Needs are things that we cannot live without, such as food and shelter.**

- **Wants are things we would like to have but are not essential.**

> *For example, you might need a new pair of shoes because your old ones are too small. But you might want a new toy because you've seen it advertised.*

It is crucial to distinguish between needs and wants to spend your money wisely.

THINK ABOUT WHETHER YOU NEED SOMETHING BEFORE YOU BUY IT. If you can wait a little while, you might be able to save up and buy it later.

Consider how much something is worth. Just because something is expensive does not mean it is a good value.

> *For example, a new pair of shoes might cost $100. But if you only wear them for a few months and then they are too small, it was not a wise purchase.*
>
> *On the other hand, a toy that costs $20 but will provide hours of fun is better value. It is helpful to consider both the price and the quality when making a purchase.*

Finally, **try to be aware of sales and discounts**. You might be able to get the same toy for $10 if you wait for a sale. Or you might be able to find a coupon for $20 off your purchase.

Keep your eyes open for these deals to save money on the things you want to buy.

Here are a few tips to help you spend money wisely:

 Buy items on sale: This is a great way to get something you want while spending less money.

 Plan ahead: If you know you are going to want something in the future, you can start saving for it now.

 Buy used items: Used items are often just as good as new items but cost less. There are often bargains to be found at garage sales and thrift stores. You can also find great deals on second-hand items online with your parent's help.

 Compare prices: It pays to shop around and compare prices before making a purchase.

 Be patient: If you can wait to buy something, you might be able to get it at a lower price or find a better deal.

By following these tips, you can learn to spend your money wisely. And remember, the best way to save money is to avoid spending it in the first place!

HOW TO SPEND MONEY ONLINE

These days, we can buy almost anything we want online. But just because we can buy something doesn't mean we should!

When you are spending money online, you need to be careful. Just like in a store, you need to consider whether you are buying something you need or if it is something you just want.

Spending online is easy and can be done with just a few clicks. But if you're not careful, you can spend a lot of money without even realizing it.

Here are a few tips to help you spend money wisely online:

① **Always ask your parents:** Before making a purchase, ask your parents or an adult if it is okay.

② **Compare prices:** Many different websites sell the same things. So it pays to shop around and compare prices before making a purchase.

③ **Only buy from reputable websites:** This is the most important rule when buying anything online. Do you know the site? Have you heard of it before? You should consider these things before giving your credit card information to any website. If you're unsure, ask your parents or another adult for help.

④ **Read the reviews:** Before you buy something, read the reviews. This will help you avoid buying something that is not worth the money.

⑤ **Look for coupon codes:** You can often find discounts and coupons online. Be sure to check for these before you make a purchase.

Following these tips can teach you to spend your money wisely online. With some care, you can find great deals and save money on the things you want to buy.

UNDERSTANDING CREDIT CARDS, DEBIT CARDS & BUY NOW PAY LATER

When you buy things online or at the shops, you will often see the option to pay with a credit or debit card. But what are these? And how do they work?

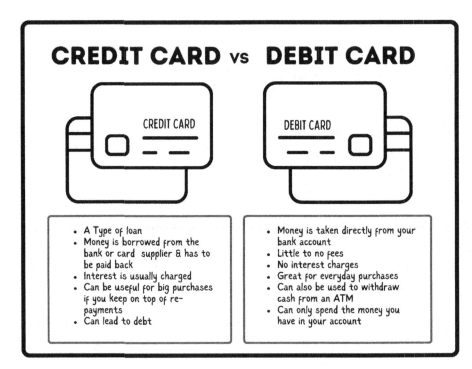

CREDIT CARD vs DEBIT CARD

CREDIT CARD
- A Type of loan
- Money is borrowed from the bank or card supplier & has to be paid back
- Interest is usually charged
- Can be useful for big purchases if you keep on top of re-payments
- Can lead to debt

DEBIT CARD
- Money is taken directly from your bank account
- Little to no fees
- No interest charges
- Great for everyday purchases
- Can also be used to withdraw cash from an ATM
- Can only spend the money you have in your account

Credit cards

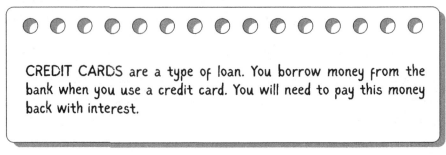

CREDIT CARDS are a type of loan. You borrow money from the bank when you use a credit card. You will need to pay this money back with interest.

If you don't pay back the money you owe, the bank or card supplier will charge you a fee. This is called interest.

> For example, imagine you spend $100 on your credit card. The bank will charge you interest; let's say it's 10%. This means you will owe the bank $110.
>
> If you don't pay this back, the bank will charge you another 10% interest on the $110. So now you owe the bank $121.

As you can see, the interest can quickly add up, and you can end up owing a lot of money to the bank. This is why you must be careful if you use a credit card.

Debit cards

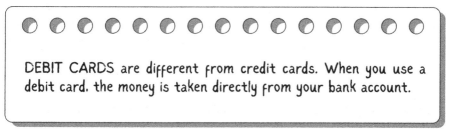

DEBIT CARDS are different from credit cards. When you use a debit card, the money is taken directly from your bank account.

This means you can only spend the money you have in your account. You cannot borrow money like you can with a credit card.

> For example, let's say you have $100 in your bank account. You use your debit card to buy something that costs $50. This means there is now $50 left in your account.

If you try to spend more than you have in your account, the transaction will be declined.

Both credit and debit cards can be used to make purchases online or in the shops. While they may look like the same bits of plastic, they are very different, and you should be careful with both of them. You don't want to end up spending more money than you have!

Here are a few things to keep in mind when using credit or debit cards:

- **Ask your parents before you use their card.**

- **Always know how much money you have in your account.** This will help you avoid spending more money than you have.

- When you are older, if you get a credit card, ensure you **understand the terms and conditions and keep on top of your monthly payments.**

- **Keep your credit or debit card in a safe place.** This will help prevent someone from stealing and using it without your permission.

Many apps now allow parents to control their child's spending. This can be a great way to help teach young adults about money and how to spend it wisely.

Buy now pay later

Even though you may not have seen it, you've probably heard of "buy now, pay later." This is where you can buy something today and pay for it over time. More and more online websites offer their customers this payment option.

> *For example, let's say you want to buy a new jacket that costs $200. The website offers you the option to pay for it over 3 months. This means you would pay $66.67 per month for 3 months.*
>
> *At the end of the 3 months, you would have paid off the jacket in full.*

This may sound like a great idea, but there are some things you should know before you do this.

First, **this is debt**. This means you are borrowing money from the company to pay for the jacket.

Second, **you will be charged interest if you don't make your payments on** time. This means you will end up paying more than the original price.

> *For example, let's say you have three months to pay for your jacket. If you pay it all in those 3 months, there is no interest to pay. This is called 'Interest-Free.' But if you don't pay it all in those 3 months and still owe $50, the company will charge you interest on that $50.*
>
> *The interest rate can be anywhere from 10% to 25%. This means your $50 debt could turn into a $60 or even a $75 debt!*

So, while "buy now, pay later" might sound like a great idea, you must be careful before using this option. Be sure you can afford the monthly payments and will pay them off within the interest-free period.

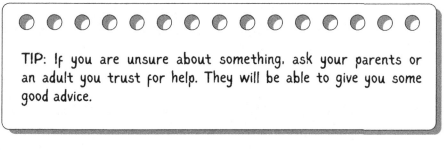

TIP: If you are unsure about something, ask your parents or an adult you trust for help. They will be able to give you some good advice.

You can learn to spend your money wisely with a bit of care. Whether using a credit card, debit card, or cash, remember to think about what you are buying and why. By doing this, you can avoid making impulsive purchases that you may later regret.

HOW TO MAKE MONEY

Now we know how to spend money wisely, let's talk about how to make money.

Making money is not always easy. When you're younger, you might rely on an allowance from your parents. But as you get older, you'll need to find ways to make your own money.

There are many ways to earn money, some of which you can do even if you're still a kid.

Money-making ideas

- **Do odd jobs:** You can earn money by doing odd jobs for your neighbors or family friends. This could include mowing lawns, washing cars, raking leaves, or shoveling snow.

- **Have a lemonade stand:** This is a great way to earn money in the summer. You only need a pitcher, some lemonade mix, and a table or stand to set up your business.

- **Do chores:** You can also earn money by doing chores around the house. This could include taking out the trash, cleaning up your room, or doing the grocery shopping.

- **Have a yard sale:** This is a great way to earn money and get rid of things you don't need anymore. You can set up a table in your front yard and sell items like clothes, toys, or books.

- **Make and sell crafts:** If you're creative, you can make things like jewelry, cards, or paintings and sell them to people. You can set up a table or sell your items online at a local market.

- **Be a pet sitter:** If you love animals, you can earn money by caring for people's pets while they are out of town. This could include feeding, walking, and playing with the pet.

- **Baby-sit:** If you're responsible and good with kids, you can earn money by babysitting for families in your neighborhood.

- **Sell your stuff:** If you've got toys or games you no longer play with, try selling them online with the help of an adult. eBay, Facebook Marketplace, Gumtree, and Craigslist are just some platforms to buy and sell second-hand goods.

These are just a few ideas to get you started. There are many other ways to make money. The important thing is to be creative and think of something you're interested in.

How to turn a money-making idea into a reality

If you have an idea about how to make money, the next step is to turn that idea into a reality.

First, you must **research and determine if there is a market for your product** or service. This means finding out if people are willing to pay for what you're offering.

Next, you need to **create a plan**. This will help you figure out what to do to get your business up and running.

Once you have a plan, you need to **start taking action**.

> *For example, say you want to wash cars in your neighborhood.*
>
> *To turn this idea into a reality, you need to do the following:*
>
> *— Do some research and figure out how much people are willing to pay for car washes.*
>
> *— Create a plan including what supplies you need and where you will wash the cars.*
>
> *— Start advertising your business by hanging up flyers or posting them online.*
>
> *— Start washing cars!*

These are just a few things you need to do to make your idea a reality. Remember **making money takes time and effort, but it is worth it**! When you have your own money, you can spend it however you like. Just be sure to follow the tips above to spend it wisely!

. . . .

HOW TO GET A JOB

Now that you know how to make money from your hobbies let's talk about how to get a job. You may not be old enough to get a job now, but it's never too early to start thinking about it!

There are many different types of jobs out there.

The best way to figure out what job is right for you is to think about what you're interested in. Do you like working with people?

Do you like animals? Do you like being outdoors? These things can help you narrow down the type of job you're looking for.

Another way to figure out what job is right for you is to think about what things you're good at. Are you good at math? Are you good at writing? Are you good at cleaning? These things can help you find a job that's a perfect fit for you.

Once you know what job you're looking for, the next step is to apply for jobs. The best way to do this is to look online or in the newspaper for job postings. You can also ask your parents or other adults if they know of any openings in their workplace.

The last step is to go for an interview. This is where you'll meet with the hiring person and tell them why you're the best person for the job.

Remember, it's never too early to start thinking about your future career! By following the tips above, you'll be on your way to finding a job you love.

OPENING YOUR FIRST BANK ACCOUNT

When you start earning money, you will need somewhere to keep it safe. This is where a bank account comes in handy!

There are different types of bank accounts, but the most common for young adults is a kids' account. This type of account is designed specifically for children and young people.

When you open a kids' account, you will usually get a card that allows you to withdraw money from cash machines (ATMs). You may also be able to set up a standing order or direct debit, which is when money is automatically transferred from your account to another account regularly.

> *For example, you could set up a standing order to pay your pocket money into your savings account each week.*

Most banks will also offer an app that you can use to check your balance and make payments.

HOW TO USE AN ATM MACHINE

An ATM machine (or cash point) is a helpful way to get cash when needed. You can take money from your account by inserting your bank card into the machine.

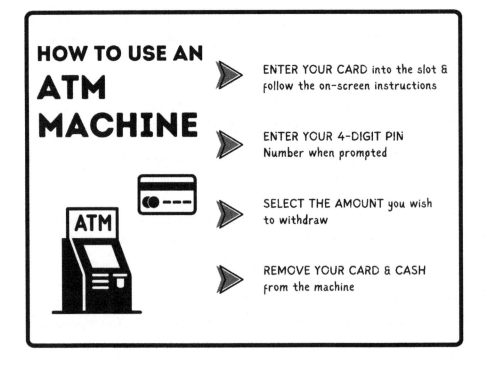

HOW TO USE AN
ATM
MACHINE

ATM

> ENTER YOUR CARD into the slot & follow the on-screen instructions

> ENTER YOUR 4-DIGIT PIN Number when prompted

> SELECT THE AMOUNT you wish to withdraw

> REMOVE YOUR CARD & CASH from the machine

Most machines will allow you to take out different amounts of cash, so you can choose how much you need. Remember that once you have taken the money out, it is gone from your account. So be sure you only take out what you need.

Some machines will also allow you to check your balance. This can be a handy way to track how much money you have in your account.

There are a few simple things you should know before using one.

First, **some ATM machines will charge you a fee for using them**. Look at the screen beforehand to see how much money they might charge you.

Second, **you need to know your PIN number**. This is the 4-digit number that you use to access your bank account.

If you don't know your PIN number, you need to contact your bank to get it. Once you have your PIN number, keep it in a safe place. You don't want anyone else to find out what it is and use your account without your permission.

Third, **you need to have your bank card with you**. This is the card that has your name and account number on it.

Most ATM machines will only accept cards with a Visa or MasterCard logo.

Finally, **take your bank card and cash** when you are finished using the machine. Do not leave them behind.

ACTIVITY

Savings Tracker

Saving money can be difficult, but if you're organized and start early on in life, it's a habit that will benefit you throughout your life. One way to help you save money is by using a savings tracker.

Try to think of something you really want that you can save towards. This could be a new pair of jeans, a top or a new games console. Now let's use the worksheet to try to save towards that goal.

1. Write what you're saving for, the amount of money you need, and the due date for when you want to hit your goal.

2. Each time you save some money towards your goal, enter the amount next to the piggy. This could be daily, weekly, or monthly.

3. Try to make saving towards your goal a regular habit. You'll hit your goal in no time.

SAVINGS TRACKER

Saving For : _____

Amount : _____   Due By : _____

Total :

Notes :_____
_____
_____

CHAPTER 7

COOKING SKILLS

Cooking is an essential life skill. It allows you to make tasty food and teaches you about math, science, and nutrition. Cooking is a great way to get creative, and it's a fun activity to do with friends or family.

With just a few basic ingredients and some basic techniques, you can learn to make a variety of dishes in no time without spending a lot of money. Plus, cooking at home is healthier than eating out. You know what's in your food and can control what you eat.

If you're not sure where to start, don't worry. There are plenty of recipes online that are easy to follow. You can also watch cooking tutorials on YouTube. With a bit of practice, you'll be able to cook delicious, healthy meals that everyone will love.

Let's get started with some basics.

- COOKING SAFELY. Cooking can be great fun, but you should always take precautions to stay safe. Only cook when you're under adult supervision, never leave cooking unattended, and always use the correct utensils.

- BASIC HYGIENE. Always wash your hands before cooking, and clean your work surfaces and utensils. This will help prevent bacteria from spreading and ensure your food is safe to eat.

- HANDLING RAW MEAT. Always wash your hands and utensils thoroughly after handling raw meat. Use a separate cutting board for meat; never put cooked food on the same plate as raw meat.

- CLEANING UP. After you've finished cooking, you need to clear up.

- FILL THE SINK WITH HOT, SOAPY WATER. Add your pots and pans and let them soak for a few minutes. Use a scrub brush to clean them off, then rinse them under hot water. Finally, dry them with a dish towel.

- MEASURING. When cooking, you need to measure your ingredients accurately. This will help ensure that your food comes out as you want it to. There are various measuring devices, such as cups, spoons, and tablespoons.

HOW TO MEASURE INGREDIENTS

For wet ingredients, such as milk or water, you'll need to use a liquid measuring cup. Pour the ingredient into the cup until it reaches the line marking the desired amount.

You'll need to weigh or use a spoon to measure dry ingredients, such as flour or sugar.

BASIC COOKING TERMS

Before you start cooking, it will help you to understand some basic cooking terms. Here are a few of the most common ones:

BASIC COOKING TERMS

SAUTE	SIMMER	GRILL
To fry food in a small amount of hot oil or butter on the stovetop.	To cook food over low heat, so the liquid is just below boiling point.	To cook food on a grill over hot coals or gas heat.
ROAST	**BOIL**	**STEAM**
To cook food in an oven at a high temperature.	To cook food in boiling water on a stovetop in a pan.	To cook food by boiling it in steam.

- **Boil:** To cook food in boiling water on a stovetop in a pan.
- **Saute:** To fry food in a small amount of hot oil or butter on the stovetop.
- **Simmer:** To cook food over low heat, so the liquid is just below boiling point.
- **Roast:** To cook food in an oven at a high temperature.
- **Steam:** To cook food by boiling it in steam.
- **Grill:** To cook food on a grill over hot coals or gas heat.

CUTTING TECHNIQUES

One of the most important things about cooking is cutting food into the correct sizes. This will ensure that your food cooks evenly and is ready to eat when you want it to be. Here are a few basic cutting techniques that you should know:

- **Cutting in half:** To cut a piece of food in half, place the knife at one end and slice down the middle.

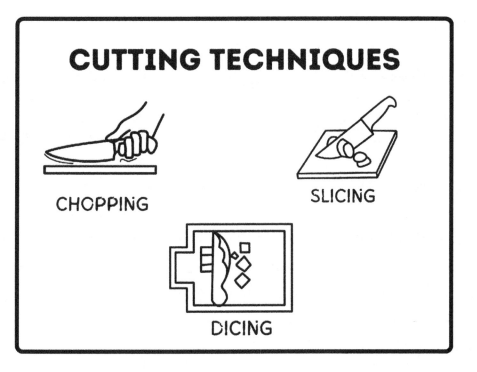

- **Dicing:** To dice a piece of food, place the knife at one end and cut it into small cubes.

- **Chopping:** To chop a piece of food, place the knife at one end and cut it into small pieces.

- **Slicing:** To slice a piece of food, place the knife on top of the food and slice down. Make sure to use a gentle motion so you don't cut yourself.

HOW TO READ A RECIPE

A recipe is a set of instructions that tells you how to cook a particular dish. It will list the ingredients you need and the steps you need to take to make the dish.

When you're reading a recipe, make sure to pay attention to the following things:

- **Ingredients:** These are the items you need to make your dish. Make sure you have all of the ingredients before you start cooking. If you don't have something, you'll need to substitute it or leave it out.

- **Time:** How long will the dish take to prepare and cook? You'll need to plan ahead to prepare your dish when you want to eat it.

- **Temperature:** What temperature should the oven be set to? What type of stove should the dish be cooked on?

- **Serving size:** How many people will this recipe serve?

Now that you've mastered the basics. With an adult, have a go at creating this delicious meal... spaghetti & meatballs with a tasty salad!

HOW TO COOK SPAGHETTI & MEATBALLS

This recipe for Spaghetti and Meatballs is a classic dish everyone will love.

SERVES 4   20+40 MIN

INGREDIENTS:

- 1 pound of ground beef
- 1/2 cup minced onion
- 1/4 cup grated Parmesan cheese
- 1 egg
- 1/4 teaspoon black pepper
- 1/4 teaspoon salt
- 1/2 cup bread crumbs
- 1 can (14.5 ounces) of crushed tomatoes
- 1/4 cup tomato sauce
- 1 teaspoon dried basil
- 1/4 teaspoon dried oregano
- 1/4 teaspoon garlic powder
- 1 pound spaghetti
- Parmesan cheese, for serving

INSTRUCTIONS:

1. In a large bowl, combine ground beef, minced onion, Parmesan cheese, egg, black pepper, and salt. Mix well.

2. Add bread crumbs and mix well.

3. Shape mixture into 1-inch balls. You should have enough for about 16 balls in total.

4. Heat some oil in a large pan on medium heat. Add your meatballs and cook them for about 10 minutes, turning them regularly, until they are brown all over. Turn off the heat and place the meatballs on a plate.

5. In a large saucepan, heat the crushed tomatoes, tomato sauce, basil, oregano, garlic powder, and pepper over medium heat until hot. Once the sauce is bubbling nicely, add your browned meatballs, turn the heat down and simmer for 10 minutes, until the sauce has thickened and the meatballs are cooked through.

6. Cook the spaghetti according to package directions in boiling water.

7. Serve the meatballs and spaghetti with Parmesan cheese or a cheese of your choice.

Enjoy your delicious Spaghetti and Meatballs!

Remember, you can adjust the recipe to suit your tastes. If you like more sauce, add more tomato sauce. Add more bread crumbs if you want your meatballs to be a little crunchier. The possibilities are endless!

Now that you know how to cook your first dish, let's try making a salad!

· ·

WALNUT AND BLUE CHEESE SALAD

This salad is excellent as a side salad but can also be the main meal.

Please note that the salad contains nuts; if you or any of your family members suffer from nut allergies, simply omit the nuts.

SERVES 4   10 MIN

SALAD INGREDIENTS:
- 2 cups lettuce (any variety), chopped
- 1 cup cherry tomatoes, halved
- 1/2 cup crumbled blue cheese
- 1/2 cup chopped walnuts
- 1/4 cup vinaigrette or make your own dressing

DRESSING INGREDIENTS:
- 2 tablespoons of olive oil
- 1 teaspoon of lime juice

- 1/2 teaspoon of mustard
- Salt and pepper to taste

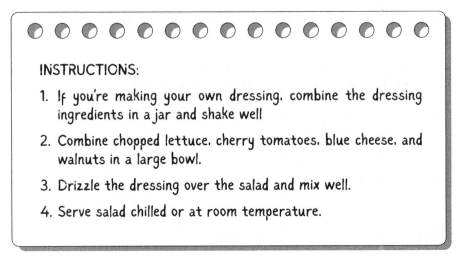

INSTRUCTIONS:

1. If you're making your own dressing, combine the dressing ingredients in a jar and shake well

2. Combine chopped lettuce, cherry tomatoes, blue cheese, and walnuts in a large bowl.

3. Drizzle the dressing over the salad and mix well.

4. Serve salad chilled or at room temperature.

Enjoy your delicious salad!

Remember, you can always add or remove ingredients to fit your own tastes. Add some cooked bacon or ham if you want a more savory salad. If you want a sweeter salad, add some dried cranberries or raisins. The possibilities are endless!

ACTIVITY

Cook a Delicious Meal

Now you know the basics of cooking, with the help of an adult, it's time to try cooking a tasty meal yourself.

1. Scan the QR code below with your camera

2. Download your FREE Cookbook for Tweens (featuring 20 easy-to-follow recipes)

3. Choose from one of the delicious breakfast, lunch, dinner, or snack recipes

4. Follow the recipe and get creative in the kitchen

5. Enjoy!

How did you get on?

What did you find tricky?

Did you enjoy it?

CHAPTER 8

HAPPINESS SKILLS

Do you wake up each day with a smile on your face? Or look forward to something during the day, and go to bed at night with a sense of achievement?

These are all habits of happy people.

⊙ ⊙ ⊙ ⊙ ⊙ ⊙ ⊙ ⊙ ⊙ ⊙ ⊙ ⊙ ⊙ ⊙ ⊙ ⊙ ⊙

But what exactly is happiness?

Happiness is a state of mind. It's not about having everything in life; it's about doing things you enjoy and being grateful for what you have.

Happiness is important because it leads to a more fulfilled life. When you're happy, you're more likely to have positive relationships and better health, and what's more, it's contagious. You're more likely to be happy when you're around happy people.

In this chapter, we'll explore happiness and what you can do to stay positive, even when things are tough. You'll learn about the power of positive thinking and how to find your happy place.

So let's get started on your journey to happiness!

HOW TO FIND THINGS YOU'RE GOOD AT

It can be challenging to find things you're good at. You may feel like you're not good at anything or that everyone is better than you. But everyone has talents and skills; it's just a matter of finding what yours are.

Hobbies are a great way to find things you're good at. If you enjoy doing something, chances are you're good at it or will become good at it. Try out different hobbies and activities until you find something you enjoy. Once you find something you're passionate about, it will be easier to find things you're good at.

Remember, it doesn't matter what other people think, be proud of the things that make you happy. It's better to be into something that makes you happy and passionate about than to be good at something that doesn't interest you.

Just believe in yourself and don't give up. Pursue your passions and do whatever it takes to find things you're good at. You'll be surprised at what you can accomplish when you set your mind to it.

Many people fear trying new things because they're afraid of failing. But it's important to remember that everyone fails at some point. **The key is to keep trying.**

You may not be good at something the first time you try it, but that doesn't mean you should stop. In fact, people often give up too quickly because they don't see results immediately. But if you stick with it, you'll eventually get better and start seeing results. **Practice makes perfect.**

Remember that everyone has to start somewhere. Pursue your passions and do whatever it takes to find something you're good at.

Another way to find things you're good at is by taking classes or joining clubs. This can help you explore new interests and meet people with similar interests. It's a great way to see what you like and don't like.

No one is good at everything. Everyone has different talents and skills. It's just a matter of finding what yours are.

HOW TO BE MORE POSITIVE

Life can be tricky sometimes. Things might not go your way, and it can be easy to get down. But it's important to remember that **you always have the power to choose how you react to things.** You can either let the bad things bring you down or choose to stay positive.

If you take a step back and look at the bigger picture, you'll see that there's always something to be grateful for.

It's important to stay positive because your attitude can affect every-thing in your life. If you're constantly negative, you'll start to see the world in a negative light. But if you're positive, you'll begin to see the good in everything. Being positive can be contagious. If you're around positive people, it can rub off on you. And before you know it, you'll be seeing the world in a different light.

One way to stay positive is by writing down three things you're grateful for every day. This can be anything from the sun shining to getting a good grade on a test. It doesn't matter how big or small; just write down three things that made you happy that day.

Another way to stay positive is to do something nice for someone else. This can be anything from holding the door open for someone to volunteering at a local shelter. When you make other people happy, it will, in turn, make you happy.

It's also important to **surround yourself with positive people**. This can be friends, family, or even co-workers. If you're constantly around negative people, it will be harder for you to stay positive. But if you're around upbeat people, it will be easier for you to see the good in things.

FIND YOUR HAPPY PLACE

Everyone needs a happy place where they can go to relax and feel at peace. For some people, it's the beach; for others, it's the mountains. It doesn't matter where it is, as long as it makes you happy.

If you don't have a happy place, there's always time to find one. Start by thinking about what makes you happy. Do you like being outdoors or indoors? Do you like being around people or being alone? Once you figure out what makes you happy, you can start looking for a place that fits those criteria.

If you're unsure where to start, try looking online for ideas. There are lots of websites and blogs that have lists of happy places. Or you can ask your friends and family if they have any suggestions.

It may not happen overnight, but don't give up if you don't find it immediately. Just keep looking, and you'll eventually find the perfect place for you. It could be at home, in your garden, on your bike, or on top of a mountain. It doesn't matter where it is, as long as it makes you happy.

Once you find it, you'll know it. And you can go there anytime you need to relax and feel at peace.

HOW TO MAKE YOUR OWN FUN

When you're a kid, it's easy to find things to do. But when you're a tween, it can be more challenging to find something that is fun and interesting.

One way to make your own fun is by trying new things. If there's something you've always wanted to do, go for it! There's no time like the present to try new things.

Another way to make your own fun is by creating your own games. If you're bored, get creative and make up your own rules. You can even invite your friends to join in on the fun.

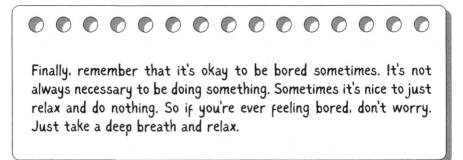

Finally, remember that it's okay to be bored sometimes. It's not always necessary to be doing something. Sometimes it's nice to just relax and do nothing. So if you're ever feeling bored, don't worry. Just take a deep breath and relax.

ACTIVITY

Gratitude Journal

One way to stay positive is to start a gratitude journal. Every day, write down three things you're grateful for.

It could be as simple as, "I'm grateful for my bed because it's so comfortable." Or, "I'm grateful for my dog." Over time, you'll start to notice that you're grateful for more and more things. And when you're feeling down, you can look back at your journal and remember all the good things in your life.

WEEKLY GRATITUDE JOURNAL

○ ○ ○ ○ ○ ○ ○
m t w t f s s

Month: _____

Monday

Tuesday

Wednesday

Thursday

Friday

Saturday

Sunday

CHAPTER 9

CARING & SHARING

When you grow older, you will start to take on responsibilities.

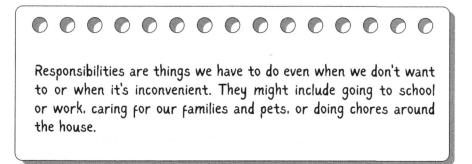

Responsibilities are things we have to do even when we don't want to or when it's inconvenient. They might include going to school or work, caring for our families and pets, or doing chores around the house.

In this chapter, we will explore how to take care of animals, look after our family, and what we can do to care for our planet.

HOW TO LOOK AFTER A PET

One of the most significant responsibilities that you might have is taking care of a pet. Pets are often like family members; they rely on us for food, water, shelter, and love.

When you take care of a pet, you are responsible for its well-being. This means ensuring it has everything it needs to be healthy and happy.

For example, if you have a dog, you will need to walk it every day, give it food and water, and take it to the vet for regular check-ups.

Cats are a bit easier to take care of than dogs, but they still need care and attention. They must be fed and have fresh water daily, and their litter box must be cleaned regularly.

Although your pet may not be able to speak, they can still communicate their needs. Over time by watching your pet, you can learn how to interpret their body language so that you begin to understand what they are trying to tell you.

For example, a wagging tail usually means that a dog is happy. In contrast, a growling noise can mean they feel threatened or angry.

Pets can teach us much about showing care and concern for others. They rely on us for their basic needs, and in return, they give us companionship and love.

HOW TO CARE FOR PLANTS

Caring for a plant is a great way to learn about responsibility. Plants rely on us for their basic needs, and we must ensure that we give them the care they need. This can be a rewarding experience, as it is satisfying to see a plant grow and thrive under your care.

How to grow your own vegetables

Growing your own food is a great way to be more environmentally friendly and save money. It's also satisfying to watch your plants grow and enjoy your labor's fruits (or vegetables). If you're interested in trying it, here are some tips on getting started.

① Choosing your vegetables

First, you'll need to choose what kind of plant you want to grow. Do you want a fruit or a vegetable? Some vegetables are easier to grow than others, so if you're a beginner, you might want to start with something like tomatoes or lettuce. Once you've decided what you want to grow, it's time to get some seeds. You can either buy them from a garden center or online.

② Planting your seeds

Once you have your seeds, it's time to plant them. You'll need some pots or planters and some potting soil. Make sure you read the instructions on the seed packet so you know how deep to plant the seeds. Once they're in the ground, water them well and put them in a sunny spot. Keep an eye on them, and water them every day or so. In a few weeks, you should start to see your plants growing!

③ Looking after your vegetable plants

Once your plants are big enough, you can transfer them to a garden bed or bigger pots. Again, make sure you read the instructions on the seed packet so you know how much space they need. Once they're in their new home, continue to water them regularly.

If you take care of your plants, you should be able to enjoy fresh fruits and vegetables all summer long!

How to look after a houseplant

If you don't have the space to grow your own vegetables, or you're not ready to take on the responsibility of a pet, then a house plant might be a good option.

○ ○ ○ ○ ○ ○ ○ ○ ○ ○ ○ ○ ○ ○ ○

Although they might not be as exciting as a puppy or a kitten, house plants can make great pets. They're low maintenance, look pretty, and can help purify the air in your home. If you're thinking of getting a house plant, here are some tips on how to take care of it.

❶ Choosing your house plant

First, you'll need to choose the right plant for your home. Some plants need a lot of sunlight, while others can thrive in low-light conditions. Look at your home and decide which room would be best for your plant. Once you've found the perfect spot, it's time to buy your plant.

❷ Looking after your house planet

When you get your plant home, it's important to check the care instructions and give it a good watering. Check the soil and ensure it's moist before putting your plant in its new pot. Once it's in its pot, give it more water and put it in its new home.

Now that your plant is settled, it's time to take care of it. Water it when the soil is dry, or according to the instructions, and give it some feed every month. You should also dust the leaves occasionally to help them stay healthy. If you take good care of your plant, it should thrive for years!

. . . .
CARING FOR THE ENVIRONMENT

As a teenager, you will have more opportunities to make a difference in the world around you. One way you can do this is by taking care of the environment.

The earth is our home, and it is vital to take care of it. Unfortunately, humans have had a negative impact on the environment in many ways. We pollute the air with harmful gases, we pollute the water with chemicals, and we destroy habitats by cutting down trees. These activities have caused many problems, such as climate change, air pollution, and water shortages.

But there are things that you can do to help. You might be thinking... what difference can I make? I'm just one person...

But every little bit helps. **If everyone plays their part, it can make a big difference.**

Here are some things that you can do to help care for the planet:

- **Reuse**

Reduce the rubbish you create by reusing things instead of throwing them away. For example, you could use an old coffee mug as a plant pot or turn an old t-shirt into a cleaning cloth.

- **Recycle**

When you recycle, you are turning waste materials into new products. This reduces the amount of rubbish that goes to landfills and helps conserve resources.

> *For example, old newspapers can be recycled into new paper, while plastic bottles can be made into fleece jackets. Try to encourage your family and friends to recycle too.*

- **Rot**

Composting is a great way to reduce the waste that goes to landfills. It involves using decaying organic matter, such as food scraps and garden waste, to create a nutrient-rich soil enhancer for your plants.

Not only does this reduce the amount of rubbish that goes into the ground, but it also provides a valuable resource for your garden. Anyone can compost; in fact, it's easy to do. All you need is a compost bin, which you can usually buy from your local garden center.

- **Refuse**

One of the best ways to reduce the amount of rubbish you create is to simply refuse things you don't need. For example, say no to plastic straws in your drinks, freebies that you know you'll never use, or plastic carrier bags.

EVERY TIME YOU REFUSE SOMETHING, YOU ARE HELPING TO REDUCE THE AMOUNT OF WASTE THAT GOES TO LANDFILLS.

● Save water

Turning the tap off when you're not using it can save a lot of water. *For example, turn the tap off when brushing your teeth while scrubbing away.*

● Save energy

You can help to save energy by turning off lights and electrical appliances when you're not using them. It only takes a second, but it can make a big difference. *For example, turn off your bedroom light when you leave the room, and unplug your phone charger when you're not using it.*

● Walk or cycle

Whenever possible, **try to walk or cycle instead of taking the car.** Not only is this good for the environment, but it's also good for your health.

● Buy local

Support your local farmers and businesses by buying locally produced food and goods. This helps reduce the energy used to transport goods from one place to another.

- **Grow your own**

You can save money and eat healthily by growing your own fruit and vegetables. It's also good for the environment because it uses no fossil fuels (energy from things like oil and coal).

We all need to do our bit to take care of planet Earth. It's the only home we have, and we need to ensure that it's a safe and healthy place for future generations. Remember, every little bit makes a difference. Small changes can have a significant impact when everyone does their bit.

- -

SHARING THE WORLD WITH OTHERS

We share the world with billions of other people and must learn to live together peacefully.

Here are some things that you can do to make the world a better place for everyone:

- **Respect other people**

It's important to respect other people, even if they are different from you. This means listening to what they say and treating them with kindness and understanding.

- **Respect other cultures**

There are many different cultures worldwide, and it's important to respect them all. This means being open-minded and tolerant of others, even if they don't share your beliefs or values.

● Stand up to discrimination

Discrimination is when people are mistreated because of their race, religion, or other factors. It's wrong, and it needs to be stopped.

If you see someone discriminated against, don't be a bystander—speak up and do something about it.

● Be an ally

An ally speaks up for others, even if they are not directly affected by the issue.

> *For example, suppose you see someone being bullied because of their race, religion, or sexuality. In that case, you can be an ally by speaking up and standing up for them.*

● Respect nature

We share the world with billions of other living things and must respect them. This means taking care of the environment and not harming or polluting the planet.

. . . .

FAMILIES

Our families are usually the people who care for us and support us the most, and we must do the same for them.

Here are some things that you can do to show your family that you love and appreciate them:

● Spend time with them

One of the best ways to show your family that you care is to simply spend time with them. This can be anything from having a meal together to going for a walk or even just sitting and talking.

● Help out around the house

Another great way to show your family that you care is to help out around the house. This could be doing the dishes, vacuuming the floor, or taking the dog for a walk.

● Be kind and respectful

It's not always easy, but try to be kind and respectful to your brothers, sisters, and parents, even when you disagree with them. This means listening to what they say and treating them respectfully.

● Say, "I love you."

Sometimes the best way to show your family that you care is to simply say, "I love you." These three words can mean so much and will let your family know you appreciate them.

ACTIVITY

Start a School Recycling Program

Recycling is a great way to help the environment, and it's something everyone can do. If you're interested in starting a recycling program at your school, here are some tips for getting started.

1. **Talk to your teacher or principal about your idea**. They'll need to approve the program before you can start.

2. **Start collecting materials.** You'll need to find a place to put the recycling bin and ensure everyone knows where it is. Paper, plastic, and metal can all be recycled. Encourage your classmates to put their recyclable materials in the bin. You can also put up signs to remind people to recycle.

3. **Take them to a recycling center.** You can usually find one at your local grocery store. Once you've recycled all your materials, you can start the process again!

CHAPTER 10

COMMUNICATION SKILLS

As you grow older and become a teenager, you'll deal with many different people, from friends and family to teachers and employers. You'll probably be faced with a lot of challenging situations too. That's why it's helpful to have good communication skills.

But what is communication exactly?

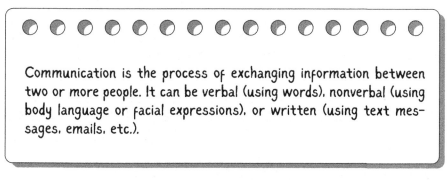

Communication is the process of exchanging information between two or more people. It can be verbal (using words), nonverbal (using body language or facial expressions), or written (using text messages, emails, etc.).

Often we think of communication as speaking and listening. But it's also important to listen and understand the other person's point of view, use body language effectively, and resolve conflicts peacefully.

This chapter will cover all of these communication skills and more. So whether you're dealing with a difficult situation or just want to chat with your friends, you'll be prepared!

HOW TO IMPROVE YOUR COMMUNICATION SKILLS

Here are some general tips on how to improve your communication skills:

1 **Listen more than you speak.** One of the best ways to improve your communication skills is to simply listen more. When you're in a conversation, try to hear what the other person is saying and understand their point of view. This is sometimes called active listening.

2 **Be firm and assertive but not aggressive.** It's good to be able to stand up for yourself and express yourself in any relationship. But it's also good practice to do this in a way that doesn't hurt the other person. When assertive, you can communicate your needs clearly and calmly without being aggressive.

3 **Don't be afraid to say "no."** It's okay to say no sometimes, especially if you're not comfortable with what the other person is asking of you. Just be sure to do it in a way that doesn't upset or offend the other person. For example, you could say, "I'm sorry, but I don't feel comfortable doing that," or "No, thank you."

4 **Be aware of your body language.** Body language is a form of nonverbal communication. It includes your facial expressions, how you hold yourself, and your eye contact. All of these things can affect the way the other person perceives you. So it's good to be aware of your body language and ensure it sends the right message.

⑤ Put your phone away. It's easy to get distracted by our phones when communicating with someone. But this can make the other person feel like they're not valued. So put your phone away and give the other person your full attention.

Before we move on to specific communication skills, let's look at some key parts of being a great communicator.

THE IMPORTANCE OF EYE CONTACT

Making eye contact is an integral part of communication. It's a way to show the other person that you're interested in what they're saying and helps build trust.

Our eyes are often the first thing people notice about us; when you enter a room or meet someone for the first time, making eye contact is a sign of confidence. It shows that you're not afraid to meet someone's gaze and are comfortable in your own skin.

Eye contact is also essential for displaying emotion. **When we make eye contact with others, we are more likely to feel connected to them.** On the other hand, avoiding eye contact can make us seem untrustworthy.

When greeting someone, look them in the eye and give them a smile. During a conversation, try to maintain eye contact with the other person. And when you're saying goodbye, make sure to end with eye contact and a friendly expression.

By making eye contact, you'll come across as more confident and trustworthy, and you'll also be able to connect with others on a deeper level.

THE IMPORTANCE OF BODY LANGUAGE

Experts agree that almost 80% of communication is nonverbal, meaning body language plays a significant role in how we communicate with others.

But what exactly is body language?

Body language is the way we use our bodies to communicate. It includes our facial expressions, how we hold ourselves, and our eye contact.

Body language can be positive or negative. Positive body language is when we use our bodies to show that we're happy, interested, and engaged in the conversation. Negative body language is when we use our bodies to show that we're bored, uncomfortable, or uninterested.

Some examples of positive body language include:

● Smiling
● Nodding your head

- Keeping an open posture
- Making eye contact

On the other hand, some examples of negative body language include:

- Crossing your arms
- Slouching
- Avoiding eye contact
- Yawning

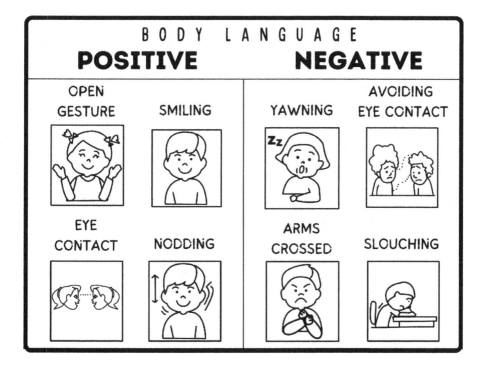

It's essential to be aware of your own body language and the body language of the person you're talking to. This will help you understand how the conversation is going and whether or not the other person is interested in what you're saying.

For example, standing with your arms crossed and your head down, you might appear angry. But if you're standing with your arms open and your head up, you might come across as friendly and approachable.

Your body language can also affect the way the other person feels. If you look at the other person and smile, they will likely feel happy. But if you're looking away and not making any eye contact, they might feel like you're not interested in what they have to say.

So it's helpful to be aware of your body language and ensure it sends the right message. The next time you're in a conversation, pay attention to your body language and see if it's conveying the message you want to send.

THE IMPORTANCE OF ACTIVE LISTENING

Active listening is a communication technique that requires you to fully engage and listen to what the other person is saying. It's important because it shows that you're interested in the conversation and value what the other person says.

Active listening requires you to do more than just hear the other person's words. It also requires you to try to understand the meaning behind those words. This means paying attention to the tone of voice, body language, and facial expressions.

It can be easy to get distracted when trying to communicate with someone. But we might miss important information or cues if we're not listening carefully.

The next time you're in a conversation, try to practice active listening. Pay attention to the other person, give them your complete focus, and listen to what they're saying.

By actively listening, you'll be able to communicate more effectively and connect with others on a deeper level.

Now let's explore some specific communication scenarios and how you can use these skills.

HOW TO TALK ON THE PHONE

It's no secret that communication is key in any relationship. But what about when you're communicating with someone over the phone? Phone conversations can be tricky, but they don't have to be! Many of us don't like talking on the phone, but it's an important life skill to learn.

Here are some tips to help you improve your phone conversation skills:

1. **Start by introducing yourself.** This may seem like a no-brainer, but it's important to remember! When you answer the phone, introduce yourself to the other person—"Hi, this is Sarah."

2. **Be aware of your tone of voice and SMILE.** The way you sound on the phone can be just as important as the words you're saying. So make sure you smile. Believe it or not, your tone of voice can be affected by your facial expressions. So if you smile

while you're talking on the phone, the other person will be able to hear it in your voice.

③ Use open-ended questions. These questions can't be answered with a simple "yes" or "no." For example, "How was your day?" or "What did you do this weekend?" Open-ended questions will help keep the conversation going and prevent it from becoming a one-word exchange of answers.

④ Avoid interrupting the other person. This is an essential conversation rule that applies to phone conversations as well. Let the other person finish what they're saying before you speak. Not only is it rude to interrupt, but it also makes it harder to follow the conversation.

⑤ Be an active listener. Just like in face-to-face conversations, really listen to what the other person is saying on the phone. This means giving the person your full attention.

⑥ Avoid distractions. It can be tempting to multi-task when you're on the phone. Still, avoid distractions like checking your messages or browsing the internet. This will help you stay focused on the conversation and prevent missing anything important.

⑦ Use positive body language. Even though the other person can't see you, they'll be able to sense your energy through the phone. So if you're slouching or rolling your eyes, they'll be able to tell. Instead, sit up straight and use positive body language to project a positive image.

⑧ End the conversation properly. This means saying goodbye in a friendly way and not just hanging up abruptly.

Communicating effectively on the phone is an important life skill that will help you in all aspects of your life, from work to personal relationships. So remember to use these tips the next time you're on the phone, and you'll make a great impression.

HOW TO BE SOCIAL IN DIFFERENT SITUATIONS

One-on-one

When talking to someone one-on-one, try to make eye contact and focus on the conversation. You can ask questions about the other person or share stories from your own life. It's also an excellent opportunity to get to know someone better.

In a group

In a group setting, be aware of the other people around you. Make sure you're not talking over anyone and that you're listening when others are talking. You can share your thoughts and opinions, but make sure to respect the views of others as well.

At a party

At a party, it's important to socialize with as many people as possible. Talk to people you know and also try to meet new people. Parties are an excellent opportunity to have some fun and let loose.

By following these tips, you'll be sure to socialize effectively in any situation.

Now that we've gone over the basics of socializing let's move on to more advanced topics.

HOW TO BE A GOOD LISTENER

Listening is an important life skill that is often underrated. We communicate with others every day, but we don't always take the time to really listen to what they're saying.

Here are some tips to help you become a better listener:

1 **Pay attention.** This means giving the other person your full attention and listening to what they're saying. Try to avoid distractions like your phone or the tv. By giving someone your full attention, you're showing them that you care about what they have to say.

2 **Show that you're listening.** You can do this by making eye contact, nodding your head, and using verbal cues like "uh-huh" and "I see."

3 **Ask questions.** Asking questions shows that you're interested in the conversation and want to know more. It also shows that you're listening to the other person's words. For example, if someone is telling you about their weekend, you could ask them what they did or how they enjoyed it.

4 **Repeat back what you've heard.** This is an excellent way to ensure you've understood the other person correctly. It also shows that you were paying attention to the conversation. For example, "So what you're saying is that you're upset because your friend didn't invite you to her birthday party."

5 **Avoid interrupting.** It can be tempting to jump in and share your own experiences or stories. Try to resist the urge and let the other person finish speaking.

6 **Avoid giving advice.** Sometimes people just want to be heard and don't necessarily want your advice. Unless they've asked for it, try to avoid giving advice and just listen to what they have to say.

By following these tips, you'll be sure to become a better listener and have more productive and enjoyable conversations with others.

Of course, not all communication is verbal, so let's look at some non-verbal scenarios.

HOW TO WRITE A THANK YOU NOTE

Thank you letters are a lovely way to show your appreciation. Whether it's a gift, an act of kindness, or simply a thank you to a party, taking the time to write a thank-you note is always appreciated.

It doesn't have to be long or overly formal and can be written by hand or typed up, whichever you feel more comfortable with. Most importantly, taking the time to write it shows that you care. It's also a great habit to get into!

Here are some tips to help you write a great thank you letter:

1. **Write it as soon as possible.** The sooner you write the note, the more sincere it will seem. If you wait too long, it becomes a hassle, and the recipient can tell.

2. **Start with a greeting.** This can be as simple as "Dear Mr./Mrs. Smith" or "Dear Uncle John."

3. **Express your gratitude.** Be specific about what you're thanking the person for. For example, "Thank you so much for the generous gift card to my favorite shop. I really appreciate it."

4. **Mention how you'll use the gift or how you enjoyed it.** For example, "I can't wait to use it to buy a new dress for my birthday party."

5. **Reiterate your thanks.** You can say something like "Thank you again" or "I'm truly grateful for your kindness."

6. **End with a closing.** If it's a close friend or family member, you can use "Love" or "With love," For a more formal letter, "Yours truly" or "Respectfully" are good choices.

If you're still stuck, here's a basic template you can adapt next time.

> *Dear (name),*
>
> *Thank you so much for (gift/act of kindness). It was (how it was used/ enjoyed). I really appreciate it. Thank you again.*
>
> *Sincerely,*
>
> *(Your name)*

By following these tips, you'll be sure to write a thank you letter that is both heartfelt and well-formed.

ACTIVITY

Write a Thank You Note

Using the examples above, write a thank you letter to a friend or family member. It could be for a specific present they gave you or a general letter of thanks for something they have done for you.

How did it make you feel sending a thank you letter?

How do you think the recipient felt when they received your letter?

CHAPTER 11

PRACTICAL SKILLS

As you become a teenager and more independent, you will be expected to take on more responsibilities, from doing household chores to fixing your bike. To help you make the transition, here are some practical skills that will come in handy:

· ·
HOW TO KEEP YOUR ROOM TIDY

As you get older, you will be expected to keep your own space tidy. An excellent way to start is by making your bed every day and putting away any clothes lying around. Then, set aside time each week to clean your room. Start by decluttering—get rid of anything you don't use or need. Then, dust all surfaces and vacuum or sweep the floor.

Of course, the best way to keep your room tidy is to keep it clean in the first place. Here are a few tips to help you:

 Hang up your clothes and put them away as soon as you take them off

2 Put away any books, toys, or games that are lying around

Make sure all surfaces are clean before you go to bed

 Wipe up any spills straight away

HOW TO DO YOUR OWN LAUNDRY

Washing clothes is a necessary but sometimes tedious chore. To make it a little easier (and to avoid ruining your clothes), here are some tips on how to do your laundry:

 Sort your clothes into piles—white, dark, and delicate. Delicates include anything that might shrink or bleed in color, like wool, silk, and denim.

 Check the labels on your clothes before you wash them. Different fabrics have different care instructions. For example, some clothes need to be washed in cold water, while others can handle hot water.

3 **Add the right amount of detergent.** Too much and your clothes will be stiff, too little and they won't come out clean.

4 **Don't overload the washing machine.** This will make it harder for your clothes to get clean and could damage the machine.

5 **Select your cycle.** If you're not sure, go with the normal cycle.

6 Once the cycle is done, immediately remove your clothes from the washing machine and **put them in the dryer, or hang them up to dry.** Otherwise, they'll start to smell.

And that's it! With a bit of practice, laundry will be a breeze.

HOW TO CHANGE A BIKE TIRE

As you get older, you'll probably use your bike more often—whether for commuting to school or just for fun. But as any bike owner knows, you will have to change a bike tire sooner or later. It's not as difficult as it might seem, and it's a good skill to know how to do.

Here's what you'll need:

- a new inner tube (make sure it's the right size for your wheel!)
- a bike pump
- a tire lever (or two)
- a patch kit (optional)

First, **you'll need to remove the wheel from the bike**. You can usually do this by loosening the bolts that hold the wheel in place. If you're unsure how to do this, consult your bike's manual.

Once the wheel is off, press the tire valve to remove any air, and then use the tire lever to pry off one side of the tire. Be careful not to puncture the inner tube!

Remove the inner tube entirely and inspect it for any holes or punctures. If you find a hole, you can try to patch it with the patch kit.

Inflate the new inner tube slightly and fit it inside the tire. Make sure it's not twisted.

Use the tire lever to put the tire back on, starting with the side you removed first. Again, be careful not to puncture the inner tube.

Inflate the tire to the correct pressure and reattach the wheel to the bike. You're now ready to hit the road!

HOW TO READ A BUS OR TRAIN TIMETABLE

Public transport can be a great way to get around, but it can also be confusing if you don't know how to read a bus or train timetable. Once you know how to read it, it's actually quite simple.

BUS TIMETABLE

FROM ST. PAUL'S CATHEDRAL TO BUCKINGHAM PALACE   FREE BUS RIDE

BUS STOPS	DAY TIMES						
ST. PAUL'S CATHEDRAL	08:34	10:12	11:45	13:45	14:30	16:30	18:45
TOWER OF LONDON	08:46	10:14	11:57	13:57	14:34	16:42	18:48
THE SHARD	08:48	10:22	11:59	13:59	14:42	16:44	18:50
TATE MODERN	08:56	10:29	12:14	14:07	14:44	16:52	18:58
LONDON EYE	09:03	10:38	12:23	14:14	14:52	16:59	19:05
WESTMINSTER	09:12	10:43	12:28	14:23	14:53	17:04	19:14
DOWNING STREET	09:17	10:49	12:34	14:28	15:08	17:13	19:19
OXFORD CIRCUS	09:30	10:56	12:41	14:34	15:15	17:19	19:25
BUCKINGHAM PALACE	09:38	11:04	12:49	14:41	15:19	17:26	19:32

Timetables are usually organized by the destinations or stops, with the times that the bus or train will arrive at each stop listed in the columns.

To figure out when the bus or train you need will arrive, first find your stop on the timetable. Then look at the column next to it to see when it is scheduled to arrive.

Remember that sometimes buses or trains can be delayed, so it's a good idea to arrive at the stop a few minutes before the scheduled arrival time.

If you're unsure, ask a staff member or another passenger. People are usually happy to help.

Now that you know how to read a bus or train timetable, you're one step closer to being a public transport pro!

ACTIVITY

Cleaning Planner

Using the room cleaning planner, list what you need to do to clean an area in the house. Note what items you might need, e.g., a vacuum, cleaning liquids, or cloths.

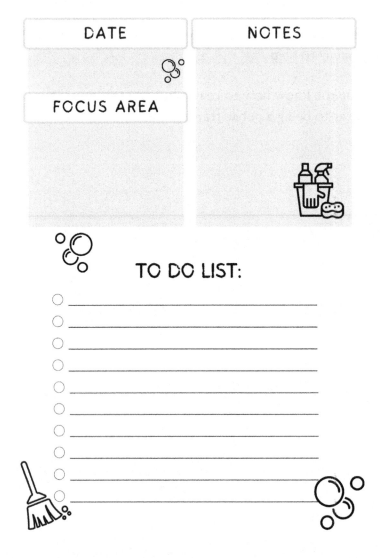

DATE	NOTES

FOCUS AREA

TO DO LIST:

○ _____
○ _____
○ _____
○ _____
○ _____
○ _____
○ _____
○ _____
○ _____
○ _____

CHAPTER 12

PERSONAL SAFETY

As you get older, you will become more independent and will probably start going places by yourself. Being aware of personal safety when you're out and about to stay safe and sound is essential.

Here are some general things you can do to stay safe when you're out and about:

1. **Be aware of your surroundings** and who or what is around you. If you feel unsafe, trust your instincts and move to a different area.

2. **Avoid walking alone at night.** If you must, walk in well-lit areas and stay in busy areas.

3. **Never accept rides from strangers.**

4. **Carry a cell phone with** you to call for help if needed.

5. **Trust your instincts.** If something doesn't feel right, it probably isn't.

6. **Make sure someone knows where you are** and who you're with.

Personal safety is important, but don't let it stop you from living your life. By following these simple tips, you can help keep yourself safe.

HOW TO USE PUBLIC TRANSPORT SAFELY

Public transport is a great way to get around, but it's important to be aware of your surroundings and take steps to stay safe.

Here are some tips for using public transport safely:

 Plan your journey, so you know which route you're going to take and where you'll get off.

 If you can **travel during daylight hours** when more people are around.

 Be aware of your belongings and keep them close to you at all times.

4 **Trust your instincts**—if something doesn't feel right, get off the bus or train and find another way home.

5 **If someone follows you, go to a busy, well-lit place and call for help.**

Following these simple tips can help ensure your journey is safe and enjoyable.

HOW TO STAY SAFE ONLINE

Just as you need to be aware of your surroundings when you're out and about, you must also be mindful of what you're doing online.

The internet is a wonderful place full of information and opportunities. You can find anything you want online, and it's a great place to connect with friends and family.

However, some risks are also associated with using the internet, and it's essential to be aware of them.

HOW TO STAY SAFE ONLINE

PRIVACY
Don't share your personal information with people you don't know.

SCAMS
Stop & think before you click on a link in an email or message.

STRANGERS
Be careful. If you see or hear something that makes you uncomfortable report it.

IT'S ALWAYS THERE
Be careful what you post online. it can be seen by lots of people and is always there.

- **Privacy:** Ensure you're not giving away too much personal information online. Don't share your address, phone number, or school name with people you don't know.

- **Scams:** There are a lot of scams online. A scam is when someone tries to get you to give them your money or personal information by pretending to be something they're not. For example, a scam might ask you to click on a link in an email or to download something, and then they'll try to steal your information.

- **Strangers:** Don't talk to strangers online. If someone you don't know starts messaging you, or if you see something that makes you uncomfortable, report it to a trusted adult.

- **It's always there:** once you post something online, it's there forever. Even if you delete it, someone might have copied or screenshot it. Be careful what you post online because many people can see it.

. . . .

HOW TO KEEP YOUR PERSONAL INFORMATION SECURE

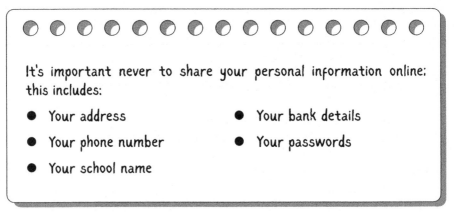

It's important never to share your personal information online; this includes:

- Your address
- Your phone number
- Your school name
- Your bank details
- Your passwords

You can take a few other steps to keep your personal information safe and secure.

 Use strong passwords: Your password should be difficult to guess, and it should be different for each account.

– Make your passwords strong

For example, instead of using your dog's name, combine your dog's name with his favorite snack and turn your password into a fun sentence.

E.g., Fidoloves5bones!

Making your password longer and using a mix of letters, numbers, and symbols makes it more difficult for someone to guess.

– Don't use easy-to-guess words like your name or your birthday.

– Try to use different passwords for different accounts. Some people use the same password for everything, but this is a bad idea because if someone guesses your password, they could access all of your accounts.

2 **Activate two-step verification:** This is an extra layer of security that you can use to protect your accounts. When you activate two-step verification, you must enter a code sent to your phone each time you try to sign in. This makes it more difficult for someone to get into your account.

3 **Update your software and apps regularly:** Keeping your software and apps up-to-date fixes any security vulnerabilities and makes it more difficult for someone to hack into your device.

4 **Be careful when you're on a shared device:** Be careful if you use a shared device, like a school computer. Always log out of your accounts after using them, and don't save your passwords.

5 **Think before you post:** Before posting something online, ask yourself if you would be happy for everyone to see it. If the answer is no, then don't post it. Remember, once you post something online, it's there forever.

6 **Be careful about what you share on social media:** Social media is a great way to stay connected with friends and family. Still, you need to be careful about what you share. Don't share personal information like your address or phone number; be careful about what you post online. Something that may seem funny or harmless today could come back to haunt you in the future.

7 **Be skeptical:** if something seems too good to be true, it probably is. Don't click on links or download files from strangers; be wary of emails asking for personal information. They may be Phishing scams. Phishing scams are emails or websites that try to get you to give away your personal information. They might look like they're from a trusted source, but they're not.

8 **Keep your online friends online:** It's a good idea only to add people you know and trust to your social media accounts. If you have online friends, be careful about what information you share and don't offer to meet up with them in person.

9 **Report anything that makes you uncomfortable:** If you see something on social media that makes you uncomfortable, or if you receive a message from someone that makes you feel unsafe, report it. The social media platform or email provider will investigate the incident and take appropriate action.

10 **Only download apps from trusted sources:** There are a lot of fake apps out there, and it can be tricky to tell the difference between a real app and a fake one. Only download apps from trusted sources, like the App Store or Google Play.

11 **Be a good digital citizen:** Digital citizenship is the way we behave online. We should be respectful of others and treat people online the way we would want to be treated ourselves. We should also obey the law online, just like in the real world.

HOW TO SPOT FAKE NEWS

Not everything you see online is true. Much of what you see may be fake news—news that is made up or inaccurate. There are several reasons why people spread fake news, but often it's done to try and influence people's opinions or to get them to buy something.

Here are some tips for how to spot fake news:

1. **Check the source or website:** Fake news often pops up on social media, so check the source before sharing it. Fake news websites often have weird or unfamiliar URLs and may not have much information about themselves. Usually, a quick Google search will reveal if the story is true or not.

2. **Check the date:** Fake news stories often get circulated repeatedly, even if they're not true. Check the date to see if the story is recent.

3. **Check the photos:** Fake news stories often use fake or stock photos. If the images in the story look strange or like they've been Photoshopped, it's probably fake news.

4. **Check the comments:** If a story is fake, you'll often see people commenting on it to say it's not true. Pay close attention to the comments to see if other people question the story's authenticity.

5. **Ask an adult:** If you're not sure if a story is true or not, ask an adult you trust for their opinion. They may have some insights that you don't.

ACTIVITY

Password Activity

Creating strong passwords helps keep you safe online and prevents scammers from accessing your personal information. Let's look at a quick activity to try to create stronger passwords:

1. Take a look at the following list of passwords and tick the ones that would be easy for someone to guess:

☐ password   ☐ abc123

☐ 1234   ☐ letmein

☐ qwerty   ☐ Trustno1!

Some passwords on the list above would be easy to guess because they are common words, have simple patterns of letters, or have few characters.

2. Now let's try to create some strong passwords using longer, memorable sentences.

   A. Write down your favorite animal

_____

   B. Write down their favorite food

_____

C. Write down your age

_____

D. Add an Uppercase and one symbol

_____

E. Now combine all of them into one sentence

_____

For example: if your favorite animal is a dog, their favorite food is bones, and you are 10 years old, your new password could be:

Dogslovebones10!

Making your password longer and using a mix of letters, numbers, and symbols makes it more difficult for someone to guess.

CHAPTER 13

EMERGENCIES & FIRST AID

One of the most important things to know when you're growing up is how to deal with emergencies. Emergencies can happen anytime, anywhere, and it's good to be prepared for them.

It could be a natural disaster, like a tornado or a hurricane. It could be a man-made disaster, like a fire. Or it could be something medical, like an injury or an illness.

No matter what kind of emergency it is, there are some basic things you can do to stay safe and help out.

Here are some tips for dealing with emergencies:

1 **If you can, stay calm:** One of the most important things you can do in an emergency is to stay calm. This will help you think clearly and make smart decisions. It will also help other people around you remain calm.

2 **Stop! Check and Assess:** Before you do anything else, stop and take a few seconds to assess the situation. Are there any dangers that you need to be aware of? Are there things that could explode or catch on fire? Is there hazardous material that you need to avoid?

③ **Call for help:** If there's an emergency and you need help, call 911 (or 999 in the UK). They'll help you get to safety and connect you with the right people who can help. The operator will ask what emergency service you need—police, fire, or ambulance. Give them your name, your address, and the type of emergency you're dealing with.

④ **Help others if it's safe to do so:** In an emergency, the people who are calm and helpful often become the most valuable. If you can, help out other people in danger or who need help.

⑤ **Follow the instructions of emergency responders:** When emergency responders arrive, they'll tell you what to do. Follow their instructions and don't try to take things into your own hands.

. . . .

A BASIC GUIDE TO FIRST AID

If someone is injured or ill, it's helpful to know some basic first aid.

First aid is the initial care you can give an injured or sick person. It's important to remember that first aid is not a substitute for professional medical care. Still, it can be lifesaving in an emergency.

But before you start first aid, you need to assess the situation. Is it safe for you to approach the person? If not, call for help.

Here are a few basic first aid techniques that everyone should know:

How to deal with bleeding

If someone is bleeding, you should try to stop the bleeding as quickly as possible.

Apply pressure to the wound with a clean cloth or bandage. Raise their arm if the bleeding is coming from their hand or fingers.

If the bleeding is severe, do not remove the object causing the bleeding (such as a knife or glass)—this could worsen the injury. In that case, call 911 and ask for an ambulance.

How to deal with choking

If someone is choking, something is stuck in their throat, and they cannot breathe. This is usually caused by food or a small object. Try to stay calm and don't panic.

Ask the person if they can speak or cough—if they can, it means that their airway is only partially blocked.

Have them try to cough up the object. If that doesn't work, stand behind them and give them five quick slaps between their shoulder blades with the heel of your hand.

If they can't speak or cough, their airway is completely blocked, and you will need to give them abdominal thrusts (also known as the Heimlich maneuver).

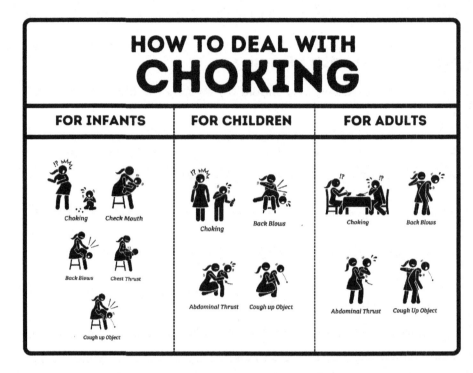

HOW TO DEAL WITH
CHOKING

FOR INFANTS	FOR CHILDREN	FOR ADULTS

To do this, stand behind the person and put your arms around their waist. Make a fist with one hand and place it between their belly button and ribs. With your other hand, grasp your fist and pull upwards—repeat this movement until the object is removed. If you can't clear the blockage, call 911 and ask for an ambulance.

How to deal with burns

Burns occur when the skin comes into contact with a hot object or substance, such as fire or boiling water. If someone has a burn, try to cool the area as quickly as possible. This will help to reduce swelling and pain.

Run cool water over the area for at least 10 minutes or until the pain eases.

If the burn is severe, or if the burn is still painful after 20 minutes, call 911 and ask for an ambulance.

How to deal with sprains or broken bones

A sprain is a stretch or tear of a ligament (the tissue that connects bone to bone). While a broken bone is a crack or break in the bone. Both injuries can be extremely painful.

If you think someone has a sprain, try to immobilize the area as much as possible. You don't want to move the injured area any more than necessary.

If you suspect a broken bone, seek medical help immediately.

If you think the person has a sprained ankle, have them prop their foot up on something and avoid putting any weight on it. If they have a sprain in their arm, have them hold it close to their body. Apply ice to the area for 20 minutes to help reduce swelling.

No one ever expects to be in a situation where they must use first aid. But hopefully, by reading this, you now feel a little more prepared if you ever need to use it.

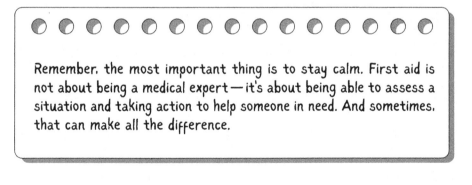

Remember, the most important thing is to stay calm. First aid is not about being a medical expert — it's about being able to assess a situation and taking action to help someone in need. And sometimes, that can make all the difference.

ACTIVITY
Emergency Role-plays

Emergencies are just that, emergencies. They can be stressful and scary, and you never know when they will happen or how you will react. But you can practice with your friends and family so that you will be prepared in the event of an emergency.

Here are a few role-play scenarios you could act out to help you prepare:

Scenario 1: One of your friends is injured at the park, and you don't know what to do.

Solution: If your friend is injured, firstly assess the injury. If a severe injury, such as a head injury, or your friend is not responding, do not try to move them. Call 911 and wait for help to arrive. If the injury is less severe, like a cut or a sprain, you can help your friend by taking them home, cleaning the wound, and applying pressure to stop the bleeding.

Scenario 2: You're at home alone when your mom falls down the stairs.

Solution: If your mom falls down the stairs, you should first call 911. Then try to help your mom by checking to see if she's responsive and by seeing if she's bleeding. If she's not responding, check for a pulse and start CPR if you know-how. If she responds, do not move her and wait for help to arrive.

Scenario 3: There's a fire in your building.

Solution: If there's a fire in your building, the first thing you should do is evacuate the building. Once you're outside, shout for help and call 911. Don't go back into the building, even if you think you can put out the fire yourself. Let the professionals handle it.

These are just a few scenarios to help you get started. **Remember never to call emergency services for jokes or pranks—only use it in real emergencies.** And always be prepared and try to stay calm in an emergency.

CHAPTER 14

ADVENTURE SKILLS

The thrill of adventure is something that many people crave. Exploring new places, meeting new people, and having new experiences is exciting. But what does it really take to be an adventurer?

There are specific skills and qualities that all adventurers possess.

Firstly, **they are brave**. Adventurers are willing to take risks and step outside of their comfort zone. They are also physically fit and have a good sense of direction.

In addition, **adventurers are resourceful**. They know how to make the most of what they have and are not afraid to get their hands dirty. They are also independent and self-reliant, able to take care of themselves in any situation.

Finally, **adventurers are curious**. They are constantly exploring and learning, always looking for new challenges. If this sounds like you, you have what it takes to be an adventurer!

Let's dig deeper into the practical skills required to be a great adventurer and how you can start learning these skills now!

HOW TO PACK FOR AN OUTDOOR TRIP

Packing for an outdoor adventure can be daunting, especially if you're new to camping or hiking. But with some planning and preparation, it doesn't have to be.

The first step is to **make a list of everything you need**. This includes all the essentials like food, water, shelter, clothing, and other items you think you might need.

Once you have your list, start packing your backpack. The key is to pack light and ensure that everything is secure and within easy reach.

Here are some tips for packing your backpack:

1 Use a lightweight backpack that is comfortable to carry.

2 Pack the heaviest items first and distribute the weight evenly.

3 Use compression sacks to reduce the size of your belongings.

4 Make sure all your gear is secure and won't fall out when you're on the move.

5 Pack essential items like food and water within easy reach.

Now that you know how to pack for an outdoor adventure, it's time to get out there and explore! Remember to be prepared, stay safe, and have fun!

HOW TO BUILD A CAMPFIRE

Building a campfire is an essential skill for any adventurer. Not only will it keep you warm and dry, but it can also be used for cooking.

You need three things for a fire to burn: Heat, Oxygen, and Fuel. This is called the FIRE TRIANGLE.

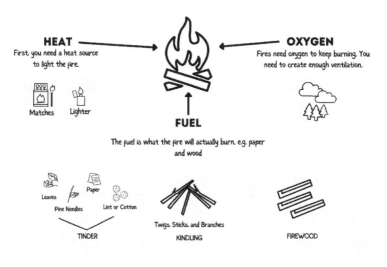

HEAT
First, you need a heat source to light the fire.

Matches   Lighter

OXYGEN
Fires need oxygen to keep burning. You need to create enough ventilation.

FUEL
The fuel is what the fire will actually burn. e.g. paper and wood

Leaves
Pine Needles
Paper
Lint or Cotton
TINDER

Twigs, Sticks, and Branches
KINDLING

FIREWOOD

5 STEPS ON HOW TO SAFELY START AND PUT OUT YOUR CAMPFIRE

1 Choose a safe location. Then make a loose pile of tinder. Don't pack them too tightly. Your fire needs airflow gaps.

2 Use the twigs, sticks and branches to build a kindling teepee around the tinder.

3 Being very careful, light the tinder from all sides using your lighter or some matches.

4 As your fire grows, add on more dry twigs and branches, and eventually, start feeding it with larger pieces of firewood. Leave some space to allow sufficient airflow.

5 To safely put out your fire, you must cut off one of the elements of the Fire Triangle. You can do it by dousing the fire with water or covering it with sand. You can also let the firewood burn out (just be sure there's no fuel surrounding the area to avoid it from catching fire again.)

Building a campfire is not as difficult as it may seem. The first step is to **find a safe location away from anything that could catch fire**. Once you have found a safe spot, gather your wood. You will need three types of wood:

1. Tinder: This is small, dry material that will catch fire easily. Examples of tinder include dry leaves, paper, and twigs.

2. Kindling: This is slightly larger than tinder and will help get the fire going. Examples of kindling include small sticks and twigs.

3. Fuel: This is the largest wood you will need and will keep the fire burning. Examples of fuel include logs and branches.

Once you have gathered your wood, it's time to start building your fire. The first step is to create a tinder nest. This is a small pile of tinder that you will use to start the fire.

Once you have your tinder nest, add some kindling on top. Then, use your matches or lighter to ignite the tinder. Once the kindling is burning, add more wood gradually until you have a roaring campfire! Remember to stay away from the flames and never leave your fire unattended.

With these tips, you'll be a campfire pro in no time!

HOW TO BUILD A DEN

One of the best things about being an adventurer is that you can build your own home away from home. And there's no better place to do this than in a den!

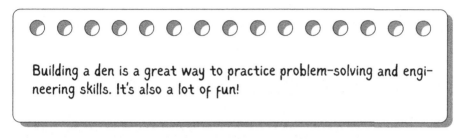

Building a den is a great way to practice problem-solving and engineering skills. It's also a lot of fun!

There are two main types of dens: natural and man-made.

MAN-MADE DEN   NATURAL DEN

Building a den is a great way to spend time with friends or family. It's also a great way to learn new skills.

How to build your natural den

Natural dens are made from materials that you find in nature, such as sticks, stones, and leaves. Building a natural shelter is a great way to reconnect with nature and your surroundings. It's also a great way to practice your problem-solving skills.

Here are some tips for building your own natural den:

 Look for a sheltered spot away from the wind and rain.

 Find a tree with low-hanging branches.

 Gather sticks and twigs and place them around the tree trunk.

 Weave smaller sticks and twigs between the larger ones to create a wall.

 Add leaves, moss, or ferns to your den for extra insulation.

 Make a roof for your den by placing sticks and branches across the top.

 Cover your roof with leaves, moss, or ferns.

Now it's time to enjoy your new home!

How to build a man-made den

Man-made dens are built using man-made materials like tarps and rope.

Here are some tips for building your own man-made den:

 Find a suitable location sheltered from the wind and rain.

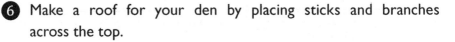 Build your frame: Use the sticks or branches to create a frame for your den.

Cover the frame: Place the tarp over it and secure it with rope.

 Make it cozy: Add leaves, moss, or ferns to your den for extra insulation.

With these tips, you'll be a Den-building pro in no time!

Of course, you can build your man-made den anywhere you have some space, but if you're going to make it indoors, here are a few things to keep in mind:

 Choose a room you can close off from the rest of the house. This will help to keep your den private and cozy.

 Place blankets, sheets, or towels over furniture to create walls.

 Add pillows and cushions for extra comfort.

 Make a roof for your den by draping a blanket or sheet over a rope or clothesline.

 Use flashlights or lanterns to light up your den at night.

Now that you know how to build a den, it's time to get creative! So grab some blankets and start creating!

HOW TO NAVIGATE USING A MAP AND COMPASS

One of the most important skills for any adventurer is navigating using a map and compass. After all, getting lost in the wilderness is not fun!

The first step is to find your location on the map. This can be done using landmarks, contour lines, or GPS coordinates.

Once you have found your location, it's time to orient the map. This means aligning the map so that it matches the direction you are facing.

Next, use your compass to find the north. Once you have found north, draw a line on the map from your location to where you want to go.

Now it's time to start walking! As you walk, check your compass and map to ensure you are still on course.

HOW TO READ ANIMAL TRACKS

One of the best ways to learn about animals is by studying their tracks. This can tell you what kind of animal it is, what it was doing, and where it was going.

The first step is to find an excellent spot to look for tracks. A sandy beach or muddy riverbank is a great place to start.

Once you have found a good spot, it's time to start looking for tracks. The best way to do this is by using a magnifying glass. This will help you to see the details of the tracks.

Once you have found some tracks, it's time to start identifying them. The best way to do this is by using a field guide. This will help you identify the animal based on the shape, size, and number of toes on the tracks.

Following these simple steps, you can read animal tracks like a pro. Happy tracking!

HOW TO FIND YOUR WAY BACK IN THE DARK

One of the best skills for any adventurer is learning how to find your way back in the dark. After all, you never know when you might find yourself in a situation where it's not safe to use a light.

There are two main ways to find your way back in the dark: using the stars and your sense of hearing.

If you want to use the stars, the first step is to find the North Star. This brightest star in the sky can be found using the Big Dipper as a guide. Once you have found the North Star, draw an imaginary line from it to the horizon. This line will point due north.

If you want to use your sense of hearing, the first step is to find a noise you can hear from a distance away. This could be a train, a plane, or even a river.

Once you have found a noise, walk towards it until you reach your destination.

And that's it! You can now find your way back in the dark. Happy exploring!

ACTIVITY

Vacation Adventures

Tick off each activity in the Vacation Adventures worksheet. Happy Exploring!

Tick off each activity as you achieve it!

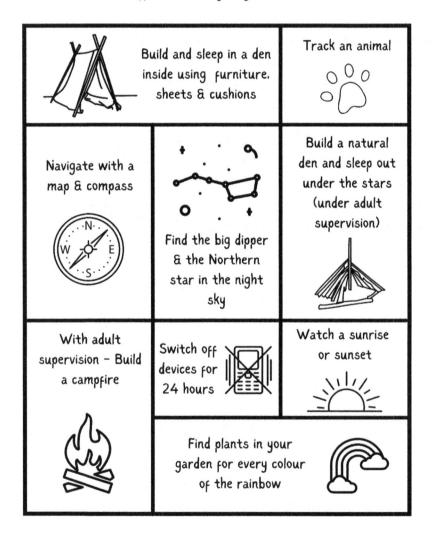

YOU'VE GOT THIS!

The pre-teen years are full of changes, not just physically but emotionally and mentally too. Having a solid foundation of life skills will make the big jump to teenagerhood that much easier. This book has taught you some valuable skills that will hopefully help you succeed in life, no matter what challenges come your way.

Many of the skills we've covered are not taught at school but will help you manage day-to-day life. For example, you'll always have to budget your money, whether buying a coffee or making a large purchase. Learning how to handle your finances now will save you so much stress in the future.

Other skills, like time management and goal setting, will help you not just in school but in every area of your life. If you can learn to manage your time efficiently and set realistic goals, you'll be able to achieve anything you put your mind to.

Remember that taking care of your physical and mental health is key to a happy and successful life. Eat healthily, exercise regularly, and make sure to take time for yourself to relax and de-stress. That includes putting your adventure skills to good use and getting outside to enjoy this wonderful world. If you can do all these things, you'll be well on your way to a bright future.

Finally, life is a journey, and there's always room to learn new things. Even if you don't feel like you need it right now, learning new skills will only benefit you in the long run. So keep your mind open, be willing to try new things, and don't be afraid to fail.

Good luck. You've got this!

Thanks for reading! I hope you enjoyed this book and that it was helpful to you. If you have any questions or want to learn more about the topics covered, feel free to reach out to me on social media or via email.

Take care of yourselves, tweens! The world is yours for the taking!

— *Your Friend, Ferne Bowe*

THANKS FOR READING MY BOOK!

I sincerely hope you enjoyed this book, and that your tween will benefit from implementing the Life Skills discussed.

I would be incredibly grateful if you could take a few seconds to leave me an honest review or a star rating on Amazon. (A star rating only takes a couple of clicks).

Your review helps other adults discover this book, and hopefully helps more tweens on their life journey.

IF YOU WOULD LIKE TO LEAVE A REVIEW

SCAN THE QR CODE BELOW TO GO DIRECTLY TO THE REVIEW PAGE.

IF YOU ENJOYED
"LIFE SKILLS FOR TWEENS"
YOU WILL LOVE
"LIFE SKILLS FOR YOUNG ADULTS"

Robin S

★★★★★ **Wonderful tips for young adults beginning their journey into adulthood!**
Reviewed in the United States on June 6, 2022
Verified Purchase

If only we were all taught these basic skills before we leave home. Unfortunately, that is not always the case. This is where a book like Life Skills comes in as an excellent teacher of learning those necessary skills! Great book, easy to understand, full of great advice.

Cara Bramlett

★★★★★ **Welcome to Adulthood!**
Reviewed in the United States on June 2, 2022
Verified Purchase

What an incredible book for a young adult transitioning to adulthood! The author covers the foundation of what is needed to transition successfully as adults. A must read for every teen!

PACKED FULL OF PRACTICAL SKILLS, HACKS & TIPS.
EVERYTHING A TEEN SHOULD KNOW BEFORE
LEAVING HOME.

GET YOUR COPY HERE: